ECHOES OF EDEN

Echoes
of
Eden

Barney Coombs

KINGSWAY PUBLICATIONS
EASTBOURNE

ISBN 0 86065 359 5

Unless otherwise indicated, biblical quotations are from
the New International Version, © New York International
Bible Society 1978.

AV = Authorized Version
crown copyright

RSV = Revised Standard Version
copyrighted 1946, 1952, © 1971, 1973 by the
Division of Christian Education of the National
Council of the Churches of Christ in the USA

NASB = New American Standard Bible
© The Lockman Foundation 1960, 1962, 1963, 1968,
1971, 1972, 1973

GNB = Good News Bible
© American Bible Society 1976

TLB = The Living Bible
© Tyndale House Publishers 1971

Front cover photo: The Topham Picture Library

Printed in Great Britain for
KINGSWAY PUBLICATIONS LTD
Lottbridge Drove, Eastbourne, E. Sussex BN23 6NT by
Richard Clay (The Chaucer Press) Ltd, Bungay, Suffolk
Typeset by Nuprint Services Ltd, Harpenden, Herts.

To my patient, loving wife Janette

Contents

Acknowledgements 9

Preface 11

1. Rebellion in the Church 13
2. Rebellion Begins in the Mind 18
3. Symptoms of Rebellion: Presumption 23
4. Symptoms of Rebellion: Fear 36
5. Symptoms of Rebellion: Independence 44
6. Symptoms of Rebellion: Overwork and Weariness 54
7. Symptoms of Rebellion: The Unbridled Tongue 66
8. Symptoms of Rebellion: Imbalance 79
9. Symptoms of Rebellion: Disobedience 93
10. Bond-Slavery: The Key to Freedom 102
11. Freedom from Rebellion: The Next Steps 114

Epilogue 126

Acknowledgements

I would like to express my thanks to all those who have helped in the writing of this book: Ann Robson, Howard Chapman, Ron Trudinger, David Freeman, Dennis Merry, Barbara Gyde, and Judy Blow.

Preface

Cy Roddenberry tells a story of boarding a Mexican flight at the little airport in Veracruz. They taxied out to the end of the runway, and then taxied back. There was a short wait, and finally the aeroplane taxied back out and took off. Once they were airborne and over the rugged mountains, Cy called for the stewardess. 'What happened back there?' 'Oh, the pilot found something wrong with the engine and brought the plane back to the ramp. He said it was too dangerous to fly.' Alarmed, Cy looked out of the window at the mountains far below and asked, 'Did they change the engine?' 'Oh no, Senor,' she replied, 'they changed the pilot!'

When our lives come under the control of Jesus Christ, not only does he become the pilot, but he begins to change the engine as well. This book takes a look at a root problem still in existence in many of us who have already changed pilots and given our lives to Christ: the root problem is rebellion.

In many committed Christians rebellion is like a mechanical fault that still surfaces and stores up problems despite the change of pilot. The following chapters are not aimed at a blatant rebel, but are an attempt to identify rebellion, as it is found in its various forms, even in sincere

Christian people. They also aim to seek from God the remedies that may lead us fully into his plan and direction for our lives. In other words: 'That we might live to the praise of his glory.'

1

Rebellion in the Church

Rebellion is like the sin of divination [witchcraft], and arrogance like the evil of idolatry (1 Sam 15:23).

A preacher's nightmare is to find himself standing before a congregation when, in the middle of his message, his mind goes totally blank. It was a Sunday evening and I was well into my sermon, speaking on how God is revealed in the beauty of his creation. From Psalm 19 I read how 'the heavens declare the glory of God' and said how the sun, the moon, the trees, the flowers, all tell us that God exists. I took a daffodil out of a nearby vase to emphasize my point. It was then that the dreaded curtain drew across my mind and the name of the flower vanished without trace. I struggled but fear filled the vacuum left by the departed word. I was greatly embarrassed and after more moments of struggle I finally laughed nervously and asked the congregation, 'What is it?' From the rear of the building an irate voice boomed, 'What do you think it is, a bloomin' cabbage?'

It had been a time of reconstruction in the church. Traditions had been challenged and the Holy Spirit was releasing people into new forms of worship. The outburst from the back was one of frustration that had, in fact, been building up for months. He was really expressing his anger at the changes in 'his' church. All that God was doing had touched something deep in that man and caused such a strong negative reaction that it drove him to it constantly.

What is this potent force that runs like a subterranean river within man's heart, bursting forth unexpectedly, far from its source? It is something inherent in all of us: something insidious, something God detests and speaks of in the strongest terms: *rebellion*.

Rebellion!

Rebellion is in the heart of Satan and characterizes all that he does in the earth. We recognize the hallmarks of his handiwork in many areas. Rebellion tears down governments only to replace them with radical alternatives that deepen many a nation's misery. Terrorism of all kinds is rampant. We see the rebellion in young people as they shake their fists in the face of any form of authority and order.

We recoil at such rebellion, recognizing Satan's hand in all of it, but then fail to see that in our lives, too, it is a fundamental problem, even though we are Christians.

God has called us to obey him. In the life of Jesus, in all that he did and taught, in his ministry and in his death, we see a total submission to the authority of his Father. His attitude demonstrated his deepest motivation, which was to please his Father, God:

> Jesus gave them this answer: 'I tell you the truth, the Son can do nothing by himself; he can do only what he sees his Father doing, because whatever the Father does the Son also does' (Jn 5:19).

> By myself I can do nothing; I judge only as I hear, and my judgment is just, for I seek not to please myself but him who sent me (Jn 5:30).

Father, if you are willing, take this cup from me; yet not my will, but yours be done (Lk 22:42).

Then I said, 'Here I am, I have come—it is written about me in the scroll. I desire to do your will, O my God; your law is within my heart' (Ps 40:7–8).

Obedience and submission are fundamental requirements that God makes of those whom he calls his own. In the Scriptures we see disobedience and rebellion continually causing havoc in the lives of individuals and playing a crucial role in the destruction of nations.

Unfortunately, in the church the words *rebel* and *obey* have not generally been popular and there has been little effective systematic teaching on them. We like to be encouraged. We like to be given a vision of who God is and his plans. We like to hear of faith, hope, courage, love and loyalty. But if, as adults, we are taught about obedience, we will often react badly, even though the rebellion inherent in all of us may be the cause of failure, mediocrity and inconsistency in our Christian lives.

The aim of this book is to help us recognize the rebellion in our own lives and hopefully to show us how to deal with it, that we might then be able to love and serve our God more effectively. It is intended to draw us closer to him by dealing with the roots of an insidious sin that robs us of power, peace and fellowship.

All rebellion is, in the end, against God. It may be the authority of a parent, employer or government that is opposed, but ultimately the conflict is with God:

Everyone must submit himself to the governing authorities, for there is no authority except that which God has established. The authorities that exist have been established by God. Consequently, he who rebels against the authority is rebelling against what God has instituted, and those who do so will bring judgment on themselves (Rom 13:1–2).

To rebel against God is the height of arrogance. Look at it this way. Look up into the heavens on a crisp winter's night—and you will see an awesome sight. The black sky sparkles with clusters of stars—the nearest of which would take us 80,000 years to reach in the fastest rocket. Our earth is one of several planets revolving around just such a small star—our sun. In our galaxy there are millions of stars each with their own planets, yet our galaxy is only one of a cluster of ten and there are millions of clusters of galaxies in the universe! The star-filled sky we gaze at is only a small corner of the universe which God spoke into being with a word! Furthermore it is still held together by that word! This display of his glory helps us glimpse his infinite, eternal and mighty nature. God created all the universe and still we pit our will against his, rebel against his authority—what arrogance this is!

A story from the life of Saul, the first king of Israel, illustrates this same arrogance and God's response to it. Saul was a good soldier, tall and handsome, appointed by God as king, but later rejected. He had previously manifested basic character flaws of moodiness, impetuosity, surliness, ill temper and jealousy. He lost his kingdom, not because of these, but because of rebellion, for disobeying what God had clearly told him to do.

He was given very precise instructions to attack the Amalekites and utterly destroy everyone and everything. With two hundred and ten thousand soldiers he set out to war, but when he attacked the enemy he spared the king and the best of the sheep, the oxen and the lambs, as well as keeping anything valuable. As they returned from battle, Samuel the prophet went out to meet Saul, who boasted that he had carried out the command of the Lord. Samuel challenged him, asking what the bleating of sheep was that he could hear. Saul immediately went on the defensive and blamed the people, saying that they had taken the animals to sacrifice to the Lord. But Samuel responded with these very famous words:

> Has the Lord as much delight in burnt offerings and sacrifices as in obeying the voice of the Lord? Behold, to obey is better than sacrifice, and to heed than the fat of rams. For rebellion is as the sin of divination [witchcraft], and insubordination [stubbornness] is as iniquity and idolatry (1 Sam 15:22–23 NASB).

See how God equates rebellion and stubbornness with witchcraft and idolatry. It is interesting to note that Saul's last sin was to consult the witch of Endor.

Some people accept their stubbornness and rebellious nature as an inevitable part of their character. We need to see how seriously God views it—as evil a sin as witchcraft. Then perhaps it will motivate us to allow the Holy Spirit to deal thoroughly with this tenacious and deep-rooted sin.

2

Rebellion Begins in the Mind

The seedbed of rebellion is in the subconscious mind. The subconscious is a great unchartered area within us. The thoughts we have concerning what we are experiencing or our past or future make up our conscious mind, but it is like the tip of an iceberg. Beneath that lies hidden the greater part, our subconscious, whose powerful effects may surprise us.

I remember a period of time when I began having a great deal of pain in my stomach. I had just left the police force and was about to go to Bible School. My doctor referred me to a consultant at a London hospital and I spent many nights of broken sleep wondering what these stomach pains could be. Perhaps they were an ulcer, or could they be something worse?

Later I arrived at the out-patients department. As I waited, I looked around at the other patients, most of whom looked very ill. Some were in wheelchairs, some had limbs in plaster. What little optimism that remained in me began to ebb away altogether, so by the time I was called in for my X-rays I was convinced I had something seriously wrong with me. Later I was called in to see the consultant who carefully scrutinized my X-rays before settling down in his chair. He peered over his spectacles and began to probe me about any worries I might have.

'None that I am aware of,' I replied, adding, 'but I am leaving my job.'

'Ah,' he said, 'I thought it would be something like that. I can find nothing physically wrong with you, Mr Coombs, and I believe the problem is in your mind.'

I was amazed that the excruciating pain in my stomach should have its origins in my mind but, reassured, I walked out of the hospital feeling terrific. The day seemed brighter, the birds were singing cheerfully, and I found myself whistling along with them. Suddenly I realized that I had no pain. I felt foolish at having had sleepless nights worrying needlessly. What I had had was a psychosomatic illness, my mind (*psyche*) ruling my body (*soma*).

I learned later that most illness begins in the mind, such is the power of the subconscious. Anxiety, frustration, tension, resentment, bitterness, loneliness, even boredom can be the cause of illness. And Christians are not exempt from the effects of the subconscious mind.

The subconscious part of the mind is like a vast library, out of which the conscious mind draws information. The problem is that the librarian in charge of the subconscious constantly offers up information that we were not seeking. It draws on our past experiences and guides our responses to what is currently happening so that some of our decisions seem strange to our conscious mind.

There have been times when I would have liked to do something, but I've said 'No' without a logical reason. Later I've realized my foolishness and wondered why I had responded in such a way. But a little pride or defence mechanism was tucked away in there. Our motives, responses, decisions and attitudes are constantly conditioned by our subconscious mind. Hundreds of our decisions every day are made in this sort of way.

Some of us become so conditioned by our subconscious mind we are like the horse used by the fire brigade to pull the fire engine and water tank. When the horse became too old and was not able to gallop fast enough they retired it, and it was bought at a very cheap price by a milk distributor, who used it to pull the milk cart. One day, the horse heard the sound of a fire alarm and took off, with milk spilling everywhere. It responded to the fire bell because it had always been conditioned to do so.

Often we act in ways governed by previous behaviour patterns—even when we know it's inappropriate. For example, I always use a certain route home from the office. One day my wife asked if I would buy a couple of loaves of bread on my way home. But the shop was out of the way and in the end, although I set off intending to get the bread, I found myself driving up to the front of our house without it. I had responded to an automatic behaviour pattern which I followed every day.

We have the same problem in the church, except that it is usually wilful. We do not like change and, because we have been doing something in a particular way for years, we feel justified in continuing, even though this resistance to change God calls rebellion.

Two-thirds of the world today is affected by the thoughts and ideas of men who are now dead—Marx, Engels, Lenin and Mao. Until recently the whole of this planet's largest nation, China, was subject to and bound by a little red book, *The Thoughts of Mao*.

What are Satan's most effective strongholds or fortresses?

The weapons we fight with are not the weapons of the world. On the contrary, they have divine power to demolish strongholds. We demolish arguments and every pretension that sets itself up against the knowledge of God, and we take captive every thought to make it obedient to Christ (2 Cor 10:4–5).

These fortresses are not primarily Communism, the Kremlin, parliaments or witches' covens. No! The strongholds of Satan lie in our minds. So we need to be aware of the enormous capacity that our subconscious has to affect our thoughts and actions. Rebellion has its roots deep in our subconscious and is a stronghold that needs dealing with.

Unfortunately we cannot examine our own subconscious minds in a thorough way. Man is incapable of adequately searching his own heart. Jeremiah says:

> The heart is more deceitful than all else and is desperately sick; who can understand it. I, the Lord, search the heart, I test the mind (Jer 17:9–10 NASB).

King David knew perfectly well that he could not read his own heart properly, so he prayed, in one of his most moving psalms:

> Search me, O God, and know my heart; try me and know my anxious thoughts; and see if there be any hurtful way in me (Ps 139:23–24 NASB).

I am convinced that God readily answers the prayer that asks for revelation.

I was once called to help a woman paralysed from the neck down. A doctor had diagnosed that the illness had a psychosomatic origin and he felt that a minister of religion might be able to help.

When I arrived, I asked God to reveal the root of the problem and the Lord gave me a word of knowledge concerning the woman's father. She then began to relate how she and her mother had been abandoned by her father. He had left to go with another woman and such was the mother's bitterness that she had taught her daughter, from the age of six, to pray asking God to punish her 'daddy'. That daughter now lay before me having carried this fortress of bitterness all her life with devastating physical consequences. She lay, a prisoner within that fortress, with God in his mercy showing her the way of escape.

I spoke to her about forgiveness and encouraged her that if she would forgive her father, God would heal her. She vehemently refused saying she could never forgive him and I had to tell her that because of this there was nothing I could do. To my knowledge she remains paralysed to this day, still bitter and suffering through her deep-seated hate.

Only God can show us our rebellion, where it lies and how we can be rid of it. If I am preserving myself and caring for my own life, leaving God in any way out of it, I am opposing the very purpose for which he created and redeemed me. We need to let God do the searching. I do not have the wisdom and ability to properly search my own heart. I need to look to the Lord for revelation. That will be the beginning of an upward road of increasing obedience to him with increasing freedom, fulfilment and glory in my life.

If the God of the universe could create millions upon millions of stars and planets and hold them all together 'by the word of his power', then he can surely show me what is lurking in the depths of my mind and reveal the rebellion that I don't realize is there.

For years I thought the major sins of life were viewing bad films, smoking and gambling. I later discovered that these were as mere pimples compared with the huge growths in my spiritual life. These larger areas had to do with motivations, responses and attitudes.

God can deal with the hidden motives of the heart. He brings a unique kind of mirror to our lives, one that shows us what he wants us to deal with next. He actually tends to cover the rest because we would be so discouraged if we saw ourselves as he sees us. Slowly, methodically, even unexpectedly, God will penetrate the deepest parts of us. It is hard and painful but the results can be tremendous.

3

Symptoms of Rebellion: Presumption

The clock on the wall had stopped. Underneath, a little sign read: 'Don't look at my face, the problem lies deeper.' Many intense or sad faces are just outward expressions of inner turmoil or distress.

If a doctor suspects something radically wrong with someone's head, for example a tumour, he will probably ask the patient about headaches, lethargy, dizziness, visual disturbances and strange behaviour or feelings. He will check a person's eyes and test for any muscular weakness. What he is looking for are symptoms or tell-tale manifestations of pressure within the brain.

We are now going to look at some symptoms of rebellion. I'm not referring, at this point, to an evil spirit but to an attitude that God wants us to be aware of in ourselves. He wants us to face what he shows us and, with his help, to deal with it.

Let us look first of all at presumption. Bob Mumford has defined this as 'Doing good things God hasn't asked us to do.' Good ideas carry no real authority and power, even when we think we are doing God's will. They can mean we are acting presumptuously, attempting to do something God never intended or equipped us to do.

Presumption is arrogance. It shows a disrespect for

authority. It is borne out of impatience and a refusal to listen.

> He who makes haste with his feet errs (Prov 19:2 NASB).

David prays in Psalm 19:

> Keep back Thy servant from presumptuous sins; let them not rule over me; then I shall be blameless, and I shall be acquitted of great transgression (v. 13 NASB).

In the previous verse he had asked, 'Who can discern his errors? Acquit me of hidden faults.'

Here is how presumption can work. Someone asks me to do a favour and I come under a subtle kind of pressure from within that needs to be watched carefully. The more insecure I am, the greater the pressure I feel to rush into some obligation or involvement. It gratifies a need for acceptance. Wanting to appear kind and to be appreciated can lead us into presumption, taking on a task God never intended us to do.

This becomes heavy and I get worn out. Jesus said that his burden is light and he meant it. Mine is heavy because I have, through presumption, become involved. Having given my word it is difficult to withdraw and admit defeat. Presumption has deluded me and I am enmeshed in a situation that results only in the frustration of joyless human endeavour. The problem is that no grace of God is supplied to carry out my commitment satisfactorily.

This is a very common kind of situation and few of us would consider it a presumptuous sin. God sees it, however, as a very serious issue. Read Deuteronomy 17:12:

> And the man who acts presumptuously by not listening to the priest who stands there to serve the Lord your God, nor to the judge, that man shall die; thus you shall purge the evil from Israel (NASB).

Another passage illustrates the seriousness of presumption:

> Nadab and Abihu, the sons of Aaron, took their respective firepans, and after putting fire in them, placed incense on it and offered strange fire before the Lord, which He had not commanded them. And fire came out from before the presence of the Lord and consumed them, and they died before the Lord (Lev 10:1–2 NASB).

There was no problem with the fire as such. But it became 'strange fire' when they did something, in God's name, and before God's people, which God had not told them to do. A sobering thought in an age when the words 'God told me...' trip off so many tongues.

Take a further example from the Bible. In the book of Joshua, chapter 9, we see that Joshua was winning great victories in the Promised Land. Jericho and Ai and other Canaanite cities had been conquered. But the Hivites who lived in the city of Gibeon decided on some crafty manoeuvring to save their skins. They arrived at Joshua's camp at Gilgal with worn-out clothing. Their bread was dry and crumbled.

'We have come from a far country,' they pleaded with the men of Israel. 'Could you please make a covenant with us?'

'You may be living in this land; how then could we make such a covenant with you?' replied the Israelites. 'Who are you and where do you come from?'

The Gibeonites then told a carefully prepared story to Joshua and his men, at the same time flattering them, and even God! But it was all a tissue of lies.

'We have come from a very far country because of the fame of the Lord your God....'

Tragically the leaders of Israel sampled 'some of their provisions' but 'did not ask for the counsel of the Lord' (v. 14 NASB). They proceeded to make a binding covenant with them. Thereafter, for generation after generation, Israel suffered at the hands of those Hivites.

Moses, in his younger days, was educated in all the learning of the Egyptians and he was a man of power in words and deeds. When he was approaching the age of forty it *entered his mind* to visit his brethren, the sons of Israel. And when he saw one of them being treated unjustly, he defended him and took vengeance for the oppressed by striking down the Egyptian. He *supposed* that his brethren understood that God was granting them deliverance through him, but they did not understand.

> When Moses was forty years old, he decided to visit his fellow Israelites. He saw one of them being ill-treated by an Egyptian, so he went to his defence and avenged him by killing the Egyptian. Moses thought that his own people would realise that God was using him to rescue them, but they did not (Acts 7:23–25).

Moses thought, 'I am God's man to deliver these oppressed people.' But he wasn't the man at that time. On the very next day when he intervened in a quarrel between the two fellow Israelites, they asked him a very significant question: 'Who made you ruler over us?' It had a dramatic effect. Moses disintegrated because God had *not* made him their ruler at this point.

So Moses ran away. He did not have God's ability and God's authority in the situation. For forty years God drained him of every last drop of his own self-ambition, arrogance and presumption. Then, when he had become 'the most humble man in all the earth' (Num 12:3) and was looking after sheep in the far side of the desert, (Ex 3:1) God said, 'Now, Moses, you're the man to bring my people out of Egypt.'

> 'Not me, Lord,' Moses reacted, 'Who am I that I should go to Pharoah?'

Forty years earlier his desire had been: 'Just let me get on with the job.' Now he pleaded, 'Not me, Lord, I can't speak properly. I won't know what to say. They won't follow me.' But God said, 'I will be with you. Tell them I AM has sent you.'

Moses now had authority. God was sending him. Signs and wonders followed. God's 'mighty hand and out-stretched arm' were manifest through him.

It sounds simple: to be totally at God's disposal and totally relying on him with no presumption whatever in going one's own way. In a sense, to those who have been drained of all rebellion, it is simple. But for most of us the great difficulty is getting to a place of submission and humility. Just think—Moses was eighty before he reached that point!

It is important that we see the essential difference between Moses at forty and Moses at eighty. At eighty he did it God's way. God's way has all the comfort, security, joy, rest and peace with it.

Let us look again at the life of Saul. The Philistines had come up to fight with Israel with '30,000 chariots and 6,000 horsemen, and people like the sand which is on the seashore.' Many of the Israelites panicked, hiding them-selves 'in caves, in thickets, in cliffs, in cellars, and in pits.' Some even ran away across the Jordan to Gad and Gilead (1 Sam 13:5–14 NASB).

Saul, however, remained in Gilgal and 'the people followed him trembling' (v.7). He waited seven days, the length of time indicated by Samuel. But Samuel was delayed and the people began to scatter. So Saul acted on his own initiative, out of fear and impatience.

'Bring to me the burnt offerings and the peace offer-ings,' he said. He began to assume the role of priest by sacrificing the burnt offering.

Samuel eventually arrived and Saul went to meet him. Saul knew that he did not have the right to 'enquire of the

Lord' in that particular manner. Only Samuel had that privilege. Unfortunately for him, this one act of presumption cost him dearly. 1 Samuel 13:13–14 says, 'You acted foolishly...you have not kept the command the Lord your God gave you...your kingdom will not endure....'

I used to wonder why God said of Saul: 'I have rejected you', and yet of David he said he was 'a man after my own heart' (Acts 13:22). There is almost a little play on words in these words, 'after my own heart'. Basically the phrase means, 'after my own character', or 'of like character to mine'. But more than this, David was in fact a man who *ran after God's heart*. In Psalm 42:1 we hear him crying:

> As the deer pants for the water brooks, so my soul pants for Thee, O God (NASB).

David sinned but he knew what it was to get to grips with himself. When Nathan faced him with his terrible sin (with Bathsheba and Uriah) he did not offer excuses but turned immediately to God in contrition and repentance. He prayed, 'Create in me a pure heart, O God, and renew a steadfast spirit within me' (Ps 51:10). And God did just that.

Saul's response was one of excuses: 'It was the people's fault,' or 'It was Samuel's fault.' He would not face himself or his sins. He tried to hide from God's all-seeing eye. David, by contrast, exposed himself further and prayed: 'Search me, O God, and know my heart...' (Ps 139:23).

It seems that David committed even grosser sins than Saul in the areas of murder and adultery. Yet what concerned God far more was the rebellion in Saul's heart. David, by and large, knew what it meant to submit to the Lord his God, to wait for God's direction and to do what he heard from God.

Presumption is pseudo-faith. It is faith without the word of the Lord. According to Romans 10:17 true 'faith comes from hearing, and hearing by the word of Christ' (NASB).

When Elijah was led by God into the contest with the prophets of Baal on Mount Carmel to prove which was the true God he did not act on his own initiative. It was not just a whim or good idea that Elijah had when he dug a ditch around the altar and poured water over it. Later he went off alone and prayed; 'I have done all these things at Thy word' (1 Kings 18:36 NASB). God had told him exactly what to do. That's why the fire fell—because God was in the whole of that Mount Carmel incident from the beginning.

When Peter, the experienced fisherman, failed to catch anything, it wasn't his idea to try the net on the other side. Instead, 'at Your bidding I will let down the nets' (Lk 5:5 NASB), and of course, there were fish.

'Noah didn't guess a flood was coming. God told him where and how and with what to build that ark, and he did what he was told.

When we are in the will of God, we receive his power, his authority and his provision. God wants to see his mighty, supernatural works performed by us and through us, but he must be the initiator, director, overseer, provider and finisher of them. He is the Alpha and Omega. And what he starts, he finishes. He is *always* successful!

Hearing God

The question I have often been asked, especially by new Christians, is a two-fold one. 'How do you hear God's voice and how can you be sure it's not simply your own active imagination?'

This is especially important when one considers God's word to Israel in Deuteronomy 8:3. 'Man does not live by bread alone, but man lives by everything that proceeds out of the mouth of the Lord' (NASB). Also Isaiah 55:3

where he says: 'Listen, that you may live' (NASB). The central issue of this book is a matter of life and death. To listen and obey God means to live, while to rebel means death. This is exactly what God said to Adam in the garden.

Although some may claim that there are no hard and fast rules, I am persuaded that there are, in fact, some good safe guidelines. First of all, the Bible is absolutely full of wise counsel and direction, especially the book of Proverbs. Dr A. W. Tozer had this to say about the Bible:

> If you would follow on to know the Lord come at once to the open Bible expecting it to speak to you. Do not come with the notion that it is a thing which you may push around at your convenience. It is more than a thing, it is a voice, a word—the very word of the living God.

Bob Mumford in his book *Take Another Look at Guidance* makes this comment: 'It is my personal conviction that some 70% of our guidance comes through the written word of God.' In Psalm 119:24 we read, 'Thy testimonies also are my delight; they are my counselors' (NASB; literally, 'the men of my counsel').

I never cease to be amazed at how much of my life is directed by the Scriptures. Again Psalm 119 says (verse 105): 'Thy word is a lamp to my feet and a light to my path' (NASB). There are many things I do or don't do simply because of what is written in God's word. It is a chart giving me direction, a compass keeping me on course, a lighthouse warning me of dangerous rocks.

One illustration comes immediately to mind. The way I used to lead the Baptist Church in Basingstoke back in the late sixties was basically a one-man ministry. The only things I didn't do were to give out the notices and play the organ! Then one day while reading Ephesians chapter 4 I noticed that God gave pastors to the church to equip the saints in such a way that *they also* could do the ministry. Out of that encounter with God through his word came much of the change that Ron Trudinger has written about in his book *Built to Last*.

Other ways God speaks

The still, small voice

God also speaks in the quietness of my spirit through my thoughts without any external stimulation. This happens especially in the early morning during what I like to call 'the twilight zone' which is between deep sleep and total consciousness. At other times it can be while taking a shower or driving the car. One particular occasion was seven days prior to going into Eastern Europe. I was driving along a country road enjoying God's creation when right out of the blue God spoke to my spirit saying, 'Don't go empty-handed. Take a new suit and new raincoat for Pastor X.' That very same evening I shared with the congregation what God had impressed upon me. One lady gave the suit and another gave the raincoat. The following day a young lady called at my home with a parcel which contained a lady's two-piece worsted suit. She told me God had clearly shown her that she was to give this to the wife of Pastor X and asked if I would be kind enough to deliver it.

The first thing I did after crossing the Iron Curtain was to visit Pastor X and give him the raincoat and suit. I shall never forget watching huge tears drop down his face, he was so overwhelmed with God's care for him. Just a few days before my arrival he had been visited by a Russian pastor whose one and only suit was threadbare. Noticing this, he was touched by compassion and had given his best suit and only raincoat, and now God had immediately replaced the old with new! I then remembered the lady's suit and proceeded to remove it from the suitcase. Once again his eyes flooded with tears. 'I cannot believe it,' he said. 'As the pastor was leaving our home to return to Russia my wife felt the Lord wanted her to give away a suit just like this one you have brought, and the Lord has replaced it for her within a week!' I was so glad I had heard and obeyed the still, small voice.

Peace—God's umpire

Set in the breastplate of the high priest in the Old Testament were two stones. One was called Urim and the other Thummin. By these stones, decisions were made. How? No one seems to know. It appears that one stone signified a Yes and the other a No.

The Old Covenant is an age of externals whereas the New Covenant has more to do with internal things. So we no longer have the two stones Urim and Thummin but rather the peace—or alternatively the disquiet—of God. Paul writes in Colossians 3:15—'Let the peace of Christ rule [literally, 'umpire'] in your hearts.'

It was already past midnight as I returned to Basingstoke from Gosport. Travelling down a long hill towards a junction at the bottom an inner voice said, 'Don't go the Alresford route, return by way of Alton!' However, I wasn't satisfied that it was God so I prayed, 'Lord if this is your voice please give me your peace. If it isn't give me a great disquiet in my spirit.' The answer was immediate; a tremendous internal churning began to trouble me. So without further question I turned left at the bottom of the hill towards Alresford which was my normal route. Two hundred yards up the road stood a young man thumbing a lift. I stopped, opened the door and surprised him with, 'I wonder what God wants me to say to you tonight.'

'That's funny,' he replied, taking his seat. 'I've just spent the last three hours talking with my girlfriend's pastor about God.'

I was able to continue the good work of explaining to him the way of God's salvation and was also able to pray with him. Without any question, Satan had not wanted me to talk with that young man, but the peace of God settled the issue and God's will was done.

The mind of Christ

Another way God speaks is through the corporate counsel of brothers and sisters. Some Bible students feel that the phrase 'the mind of Christ' used by Paul in 1 Corinthians 2:16 is not something arrived at solely by the individual but by a group of people. Poor is the pastor who has no spiritual elders or deacons. Poor also is the man who has them but doesn't make room for their counsel.

Visions, dreams and angels

The normal way God instructed prophets in the Old Testament was through visions and dreams. He told Aaron and Miriam concerning Moses that his communication with him face to face was unusual. He normally made himself known through a vision or a dream which he later described as 'dark sayings'.

Dreams and visions figured prominently around the birth and early years of Jesus. It was in a dream that the angel of the Lord informed Joseph about the birth. The Magi, having worshipped Jesus and given him their gifts, were warned in a dream not to return to Herod or tell him where Jesus was. It was in a dream that Joseph was told by the angel to flee to Egypt. Another dream was used to tell him when to return. Yet another dream told him not to settle in Judea but in the regions of Galilee.

Peter proclaimed on the day of Pentecost that by way of fulfilling Joel's prophecy young men would see visions and old men would dream dreams (Acts 2). It was in a vision that an angel prompted Cornelius to send for Peter, and another vision was given to Peter instructing him to share the gospel with a Gentile. Paul was encouraged and fortified through a vision to go on speaking at Corinth in spite of intense opposition. In this he was assured by God that no harm could befall him, and on the strength of that vision Paul stayed there for eighteen months. It is clear that not only in New Testament times but down through the ages God has spoken through dreams and visions, frequently using angels as messengers in them.

A word fitly spoken

Proverbs 25:11 says:

> Like apples of gold in settings of silver is a word spoken in right circumstances. Like an earring of gold and an ornament of fine gold is a wise reprover to a listening ear (NASB).

In the book of Kings we read the story of Naaman, the proud army commander, who visited God's prophet Elijah that God might heal him of leprosy. Naaman took offence when Elijah's message was sent via a slave that if he would wash himself seven times in the River Jordan he would be cleansed. As he was fuming with pride, his own servant came to him and said, 'My father, had the prophet told you to do some great thing would you not have done it? How much more then, when he says to you, "Wash, and be clean"' (2 Kings 5:13 NASB). Naaman heard this word of reproof 'fitly spoken' and his obedience brought him healing.

Many times God has spoken powerfully to me through individuals. Some of them have been unlikely instruments in God's hands and frequently they have been unaware God was using them. On one such occasion I was sharing the ministry of a leaders' conference in New Zealand with my dear friend Bryn Jones. Late one night he and I had a disagreement over what I should be teaching. I felt strongly that I was right and went to bed determined to do as I thought best. The following morning I received a letter from my wife which included a note from my daughter Rachel who was aged six at the time. It was the usual sort of letter a child writes. 'The sky is blue, the grass is green. Tigger the rabbit is happy' and then she had inserted two Scripture verses: 'The Lord is my shepherd' and 'For thou shalt obey the voice of the Lord your God.' You could have knocked me over with a rolling pin! Jeremiah 23:29 (AV) says, 'Is not my word . . . like a hammer that breaketh the rocks?' Well, it broke me that morning and resulted in me doing as Bryn had suggested. 'Faithful are the wounds of a friend' (Prov 27:6). On this occasion the friend was my own little girl.

One word of caution is in order, however. I know some people seem to have received significant guidance from opening the Bible at random, and putting their finger on a verse, or with tweezers pulling a rolled-up paper out of a promise box to claim the verse for themselves. But it is generally accepted among leaders that this is spiritually unhealthy. Getting to know God cannot be hurried. It takes time.

4

Symptoms of Rebellion: Fear

To fear God is good. Fear is that awesome respect for his majesty and power that causes us to listen and want to please him. It is the beginning of wisdom.

There is a fear, too, that comes in times of real danger and causes adrenaline to be pumped immediately through our bodies, preparing us to take fast action that may save our life or the lives of others. However, there are also fears that do not come from God and which can indicate rebellion.

One of the biggest surprises I have ever experienced as a student of God's word was the discovery that heading the list of those condemned to the lake of fire was 'the fearful' followed by the unbelieving (Rev 21:8 AV). The list also includes murderers, sorcerers as well as idolaters. I had never thought to include 'the fearful' alongside murderers.

Why is fear so obnoxious to God? The implication of fear and worry is: 'I cannot really trust you, God, although I know you're the Creator of the universe. I can't trust you to concern yourself with me. I feel I can do it better myself. Perhaps you do care for me, but it isn't adequate. You need help from me; my worry, my anxiety, my fear.' I remember the first time I went up in an aeroplane. My anxieties were of no help to the pilot. Neither does my anxiety help God.

Fear incites us to misjudge others

Jesus and his disciples came to a village where a woman named Martha opened her home to him. She had a sister called Mary, who sat at the Lord's feet listening to what he said. But Martha was distracted by all the preparations that had to be made. She came to Jesus asking him, in effect, to rebuke Mary for not being busy with the preparations for his meal. Jesus, however, gently spoke to Martha's distracted worry and praised Mary for 'choosing what is better' (Lk 10:38–42).

Some of our frantic serving is a 'cop-out' or release from our inner worries or tensions. Martha was making sure everything was just right but she was perhaps more concerned with what people would think if all was not perfect. The pressure was on her and the fear of what others would think drove her on. The fear never gets satisfied and, moreover, as with Martha, it leads us to put pressure on others.

The chief object of fear is man

I once knew a little elderly lady who wanted to be baptized. 'But what will they say?' she asked. I said, 'Who's "they"? Is it your next-door neighbours?' 'No, I am very friendly with my neighbours....' 'Well,' I said, 'is it the other folk in the village?' 'No.' 'Well then,' I said, 'who is it?' Looking bewildered, she replied with a plaintive cry, 'I don't know.' Illogical, yes, but it brought confusion and it was not of God. Proverbs 29:25 says that 'Fear of man will prove to be a snare': a trap that grips—clamps on to—your heart and mind.

God promises that his peace will 'guard our hearts and

minds in Christ Jesus' (Phil 4:7). This is God's antidote to fear.

There was a time when Isaac and his wife Rebekah were in the Philistine town of Gerar (Gen 26). Rebekah was very beautiful and Isaac became fearful that the king, Abimelech, or some of his men, would kill him in order to possess Rebekah. It was the same situation, in the same place, that his father Abraham had faced a generation before. Unfortunately Isaac, too, responded badly to this fear of men and made Rebekah pose as his sister. The lie was uncovered and, when confronted, Isaac admitted his motive was to protect himself. The fear of man had snared him.

Fear is a major factor in disobedience. In Numbers 13:19–28 we read of the incident where the Israelites sent spies to report on the land. Moses picked twelve men and ten came back with frightening reports of giants in the land and impregnable walled cities. Only Caleb and Joshua were positive about the situation. They saw the same land but reported on its beauty and had faith that with God's help and strength, they could overcome the enemies in the land.

The people listened to the pessimistic report and responded out of the fear that had gripped their hearts. Ultimately that fearful generation had to live out their lives wandering in the wilderness. Only Caleb and Joshua went in, leading the succeeding generation.

The people had taken their eyes off God. They had ignored the fact that God had so recently miraculously delivered them out of Egypt and wiped out their enemies on that occasion. God had faithfully led them in the desert, by day and by night, but still they refused to trust God. In the Scriptures they are described as a people who rebelled against the Holy One of Israel.

Fear is constantly a barrier to God's people, preventing them from obeying the promptings of his Holy Spirit. The fear of men is often only the fear of what others might think yet still it hinders us bringing a prophetic word, praying publicly or speaking openly about what God has done in our lives. This fear, for some, totally inhibits the Spirit moving through them to bless others.

> But when they arrest you, do not worry about what to say or how to say it. At that time you will be given what to say, for it will not be you speaking, but the Spirit of your Father speaking through you (Mt 10:19–20).

In recent years I have firmly decided, when entering a stressful, confronting situation, to refuse to allow my emotions to rule that situation. God has promised to give us the words we need so I resist the temptation to ruminate on all that could be said and what my answers should be. My preparation is to put my trust in the Lord. And even in situations where I know false things have been spoken against me, God encourages me to trust him.

Without any doubt, all of us *will* have unkind and untruthful things said about us. We all have our fair share of this sort of treatment. And if the devil can get us worrying, defending and vindicating ourselves, he is happy. He'll give us even more to worry about! But fear is sin. God commands us not to fear. At the same time he both warns and encourages us:

> So do not be afraid of them. There is nothing concealed that will not be disclosed, or hidden that will not be made known. What I tell you in the dark, speak in the daylight; what is whispered in your ear, proclaim from the housetops. Do not be afraid of those who kill the body but cannot kill the soul. Rather, be afraid of the one who can destroy both soul and body in hell (Mt 10:26–28).

The 'fear of man' is described as fear that has with it a torment which, perhaps, aptly describes a person's experience of this fear and indicates where its origins lie

Fear is also an insult to the character of God. In 1 Kings 18:7–12, we read:

> As Obadiah was walking along, Elijah met him. Obadiah recognised him, bowed down to the ground, and said, 'Is it really you, my lord Elijah?' 'Yes,' he replied. 'Go tell your master, "Elijah is here."' 'What have I done wrong,' asked Obadiah, 'that you are handing your servant over to Ahab to be put to death? As surely as the Lord your God lives, there is not a nation or kingdom where my master has not sent someone to look for you. And whenever a nation or kingdom claimed you were not there, he made them swear they could not find you. But now you tell me to go to my master and say, "Elijah is here." I don't know where the Spirit of the Lord may carry you when I leave you. If I go and tell Ahab and he doesn't find you, he will kill me. Yet I your servant have worshipped the Lord since my youth.'

Obadiah was a good man but he was only expressing fear and in doing so was insulting both the integrity of God and Elijah, God's special messenger.

It is similar to the fear some have of the baptism in the Holy Spirit. He is sent to us from the loving hand of our heavenly Father and we are often fearful of accepting this gift, this provision from God. People even resist speaking in tongues, 'in case it comes from an evil spirit'. How this attitude must grieve God.

Fear is a sign of the times

> There will be signs in the sun, moon and stars. On the earth, nations will be in anguish and perplexity at the roaring and tossing of the sea (Lk 21:25).

We need to be ready for the time of shaking so that we are part of that which cannot be shaken. That which cannot be shaken is the kingdom of God which includes the immovable church of the living God. We are an integral part of an impregnable church.

Confusion, a major cause of anxiety, often comes out of divided loyalties. We need to be a people totally committed to the kingdom of God and allow him to deal with fears and despair which are not of that kingdom.

God commands us not to be afraid

This is not an option. God speaks against all worry. In Philippians 4:6 we read: 'Do not be anxious about anything.' That's an all-embracing, blanket statement for whatever could cause worry! So worrying and being anxious is an act of disobedience.

I knew a man who had a fear of cancer. Although he was told thousands of times that one does not contract cancer from ordinary dust in buildings, he would come home every day from work, undress totally in the hallway and put on completely clean clothing. This happened every single day. Every day his clothes were washed. Even when his wife came home from the hospital after having a baby, she and the child had to have a thorough bath before they could proceed into the rest of the house for fear that they would contaminate it. You can imagine the pressure, day after day, year after year. No one, including me, could come into the house because we might bring in cancer. Somehow that house was the only safe place in which he could live. Everywhere else, fear plagued him. Unfortunately, the constant gnawing of this fear would, of course, be much more likely to cause cancer than any dirt or dust. I know this is an extreme example, but not uncommon.

I have known many who have adequate finances for the immediate future but constantly live in dread that in the distant future they may be in need. But 'a need is not a need until you need it.' And Jesus said:

> Do not be anxious for tomorrow; for tomorrow will care for itself. Each day has enough trouble of its own (Mt 6:34 NASB).

God has given us the ability to cope with each day at a time. Someone has said that today is the tomorrow we worried about yesterday.

Look what Jesus says about worry:

> Who of you by worrying can add a single hour to his life?...So do not worry, saying, 'What shall we eat?' or 'What shall we drink?' or 'What shall we wear?' For the pagans run after all these things, and your heavenly Father knows that you need them (Mt 6:27, 31–32).

Jesus is, in effect, saying that worry is no help at all. Our source of provision is a God who cares for us and whose mercies are new every morning.

The fear of the Lord is the answer

The reason God encourages us to live in the fear of him is because he knows it is the key to peace of mind. So many of his wonderful promises begin with a fear of God that keeps life in its true perspective.

> The fear of the Lord is the beginning of wisdom (Prov 9:10).

> The fear of the Lord prolongs life (Prov 10:27 NASB).

> In the fear of the Lord there is strong confidence (Prov 14:26 NASB).

> The reward of humility and the fear of the Lord are riches, honor and life (Prov 22:4 NASB).

> The man who fears the Lord...will abide in prosperity, and his descendants will inherit the land. The secret of the Lord is for those who fear Him and He will make them know His covenant (Ps 25:12–14 NASB).

There are many other such statements. Instead of missing them out I encourage you to take time to read the following quotes carefully and discover for yourself the promises God makes to those who fear him:

> The angel of the Lord encamps around those who fear him, and he delivers them. Taste and see that the Lord is good; blessed is the man who takes refuge in him. Fear the Lord you his saints, for those who fear him lack nothing (Ps 34:7–9).

> How great is your goodness, which you have stored up for those who fear you, which you bestow in the sight of men on those who take refuge in you (Ps 31:19).

> He provides food for those who fear him; he remembers his covenant for ever (Ps 111:5).

In conclusion I will quote from Psalm 112 (TLB):

> Praise the Lord! For all who fear God and trust in him are blessed beyond expression. Yes, happy is the man who delights in doing his commands.
>
> His children shall be honoured everywhere, for good men's sons have a special heritage. He himself shall be wealthy, and his good deeds will never be forgotten. When darkness overtakes him, light will come bursting in. He is kind and merciful —and all goes well for the generous man who conducts his business fairly.
>
> Such a man will not be overthrown by evil circumstances. God's constant care of him will make a deep impression on all who see it. He does not fear bad news, nor live in dread of what may happen. For he is settled in his mind that Jehovah will take care of him. That is why he is not afraid, but can calmly face his foes. He gives generously to those in need. His deeds will never be forgotten. He shall have influence and honour.
>
> Evil-minded men will be infuriated when they see all this; they will gnash their teeth in anger and slink away, their hopes thwarted (vv. 1–8).

5

Symptoms of Rebellion: Independence

A woman in our congregation related the following dream:

> I saw many people from our fellowship and others I didn't
> know mingling together in a big house on a rocky seashore.
> We were singing and dancing together and the place was full
> of joy. Then I looked out from the huge picture window and
> saw that the sky had turned ominously dark and a huge storm
> was brewing. Soon the waves of the sea began to beat against
> the lodge we were in. I was blessed to realize that none of us
> seemed to have fear, but calmly walked through adjacent
> bushes and woods to higher ground behind the house. But
> one man fell behind the rest. He wasn't old or disabled, but he
> just stood on a huge boulder and watched the rising sea.
> Watching him, I sensed that he was careless. He seemed to
> think he was on a rock, but it wasn't the real Rock—just an
> insecure boulder. I called to warn him but he paid no atten-
> tion. Then I saw the waves surge forward, overturn the
> boulder and sweep the man away.

That dream speaks to me of independence. What is
independence? It is 'doing your own thing.' These would
be familiar declarations of independence: 'I'm not going
to join a house-group,' 'No one's going to tell me what to
do,' 'I don't need anyone laying hands on me,' 'All I need
is the Lord.'

Then there's the more subtle kind: 'Oh, shucks, I didn't want to trouble you with my little problems,' or 'Well, I would have phoned in, but I was ever so busy completing the final details of our move up-country,' or 'I had such a clear word from God that I didn't need to consult anyone else.'

Then there is a superficial, cosmetic submission where actions are taken with no discussion, but the pastor is told eventually 'to let you know what I'm doing, as I like to be submissive,' but no real room is left for any effective counselling.

Further, when someone makes a kind of boast by saying, 'I've really been independent all my life,' he is saying in effect, 'I've been rebellious all my life.' A good look at Scripture will show that 'doing your own thing' or 'turning, every one, to his own way' is really rebellion, and is sin.

Independence destroys fellowship

The word 'fellowship', (*koinonia* in the original Greek of the New Testament) means sharing and mutual participation. For example, you cannot break bread and observe the Lord's table on your own. It's essential to have at least one other person to share it.

I can recall when my wife and I were in Nepal taking some special meetings with a missionary group. All the staff were asked to be there. But one person decided that he would spend that week 'in the word,' upstairs in his room. That was independence. It was not many weeks before that young man fell into disgrace and had to leave.

A pastor visited a member of his congregation. She had not been attending any meetings for several months. As they sat chatting by the fireside, she declared that she was getting on fine with the Lord, praying and reading the Bible. The pastor took a live piece of coal from the brightly burning fire in the grate, and laid it aside on its own. Very soon the coal turned from bright red to orange to grey and black—cold and dead. That was enough to convince the woman that she could not do without the rest of the body of Christ.

I remember a pastor speaking about a couple in his fellowship. He had felt quite close to them, even travelling with the husband for three or four days to be a companion to him during a special examination he had to take. Little did the pastor know that the couple had been secretly gathering a congregation in their home and in fact the following Monday after the trip the couple had arranged for the whole group to leave the church and begin their own meetings. All the time the pastor had been away sharing and having fellowship with the man, at some cost in time and effort, yet nothing had been mentioned. The man and his group left creating a painful split.

I have also observed that independent people tend to be secretive. God wants his people to walk in the light with one another and not keep secrets. We read in 1 John 1:7:

> If we walk in the light, as he is in the light, we have fellowship with one another, and the blood of Jesus his Son, purifies [goes on cleansing] us from all sin.

We may be misunderstood by some, but if the intention of our heart is to please God and make room for sharing and participation in the body of Christ, then we have the guarantee of God's protection.

Often when Christians share together, they only share strengths. This is true especially of leaders and ministers. They tend to recount only the blessings and the times God has used them. That is not true fellowship.

Amongst the leadership teams in our congregations some of our best times of fellowship have been when one or another of us has walked in the light and opened his heart. When we come in weakness and share some deep need, others are able to minister to us.

Independence robs the church of body ministry

Therefore, I urge you, brothers, in view of God's mercy, to offer your bodies as living sacrifices, holy and pleasing to God—which is your spiritual worship. Do not conform any longer to the pattern of this world, but be transformed by the renewing of your mind. Then you will be able to test and approve what God's will is—his good, pleasing and perfect will.

For by the grace given me I say to every one of you: Do not think of yourself more highly than you ought, but rather think of yourself with sober judgment, in accordance with the measure of faith God has given you. Just as each of us has one body with many members, and these members do not all have the same function, so in Christ we who are many form one body, and each member belongs to all the others. We have different gifts, according to the grace given us. If a man's gift is prophesying, let him use it in proportion to his faith. If it is serving, let him serve; if it is teaching, let him teach; if it is encouraging, let him encourage; if it is contributing to the needs of others, let him give generously; if it is leadership, let him govern diligently; if it is showing mercy, let him do it cheerfully.

Love must be sincere. Hate what is evil; cling to what is good. Be devoted to one another in brotherly love. Honour one another above yourselves. Never be lacking in zeal, but keep your spiritual fervour, serving the Lord. Be joyful in hope, patient in affliction, faithful in prayer. Share with God's people who are in need. Practise hospitality (Rom 12:1–13).

This scripture describes what is often called 'body ministry'. I believe God deliberately created men with in-built needs, pockets of emptiness, inabilities and inefficiencies. It was his express intention that we should need one another in the body of Christ. No man is complete in himself. Adam, though a perfect creation of God was not complete in himself. So God brought Eve into the world to meet Adam's need.

When a man does not need his brothers and sisters to fill those God-given vacuums in himself, he rebels against God's will and purpose. Independence is rebellion against God's provision for a full life.

Independence harms marriage

In Genesis 2:24 God said, 'They will become one flesh.' I discovered after many years of marriage that there were areas of my life that I was secretive about with my wife. For example, when I first went to Canada, I began to play golf. It cost $1.00 each week to hire a golf trolley. One day at a shopping centre, carts were being offered at $19.00. I worked out that if I played golf once a week it would certainly be worthwhile buying it, so I did, but somehow when I arrived home, I hesitated telling my wife and I kept quiet about the purchase for a while. Later I announced breezily about buying the golf cart. The news was not met with great joy, and in fact, I immediately sensed a shadow which I felt was perhaps disapproval over the purchase. Self-pity set in as I began to think about her reaction, and about all that I had unbegrudgingly bought for her. I said nothing.

Later I found myself counselling another couple and the wife shared about her husband being secretive, giving some penetrating examples. I listened, becoming more uncomfortable as God began to speak to me.

As soon as I arrived home that night, I asked Janette about her reaction to the golf cart and sure enough discovered that the cause had been my lack of openness about buying it. In the ensuing days God began to show me just how much of my life I had kept close to myself. I was shaken by the extent of this sort of independence in my marriage and resolved that it would change.

Men tend to be the worst offenders in this area. It is even considered, traditionally, a part of 'manliness' to be secretive in this way, but God planned it that we should share our lives fully with our wives.

The same applies to the family in general. We need to keep our communication channels and our hearts open to one another. If we act independently, especially when it involves children who are young adults, we rob one another of fellowship.

> Husbands, love your wives, just as Christ loved the church and gave himself up for her (Eph 5:25).

This is a very familiar passage. In fact, we have probably heard it so many times it has lost its meaning for many of us. Husbands, do we give ourselves to our wives and love them with the same quality of love that Jesus has for us?

In the same passage, it speaks to wives saying, 'submit to your husbands as to the Lord.' Many women will deceive themselves that they are submissive to God, whilst refusing to accept the headship of their husbands. It is a double standard. A fair guide is that a woman's submission to her husband is the measure of her real submission to the Lord. This may help in discerning if rebellion really lurks in the heart.

Independence is a rejection of God's delegated authority

What is this 'delegated authority?' It is God speaking to us through those whom he has set over us in the body of Christ. Let me give an example of independence from this authority.

A pastor in England told me of a couple who came to him two weeks before they were due to emigrate to Australia. Everything had been arranged. They said to their pastor: 'In two weeks time, we are emigrating to Australia. We would really appreciate your counsel in the matter and your blessing.' At this stage, nothing could be spoken to in the situation and the pastor was faced with a fait accompli.

Knowing the people concerned I said that I felt they would be back within the year. The pastor felt it was unlikely because they would then lose the financial assistance they were receiving from the Australian government to help them move. But sure enough they returned and lost virtually everything they had. They had begun with their own beautifully furnished home but now had to rent a home and borrow essential furniture.

Their misery occurred because of their rebellion. They had acted independently of God's delegated authority in their lives and God did not bless them.

Some people speak to their pastor about a decision, not to seek his advice or confirmation regarding the matter, but just to clear their own conscience.

A Christian girl came to me one day. She had become engaged to a non-Christian man and wanted me to conduct their marriage service and give them our blessing. I looked to the Lord for wisdom and felt God prompted me to ask her what she would do if she were the pastor and someone came to her in the situation.

'Would you marry them?' I asked.

She thought for quite a while before answering, 'No, I don't think I could.'

'Well, my dear', I said, 'neither can I'. Sadly, she did marry that person and has not really walked with God since.

The early church knew what it was to live under God's delegated authority and submit their lives to it. We read in 1 Thessalonians 5:12–13:

Now, we ask you, brothers, to respect those who work hard

among you, who are over you in the Lord and who admonish
you. Hold them in the highest regard in love because of their
work. Live in peace with one another.

And Hebrews 13:17 reads:

> Obey your leaders and submit to their authority. They keep
> watch over you as men who must give an account. Obey them
> so that their work will be a joy, not a burden, for that would
> be of no advantage to you.

God speaks over and over again about being and
belonging together and about unity:

> How good and pleasant it is when brothers live together in
> unity! (Ps 133:1).

> The Lord God said, 'It is not good for the man to be alone. I
> will make a helper suitable for him' (Gen 2:18).

> All men will know that you are my disciples if you love one
> another (Jn 13:35).

> For where two or three come together in my name, there am I
> with them (Mt 18:20).

> All the believers were together (Acts 2:44).

> All the believers were one in heart and mind (Acts 4:32).

> And let us consider how we may spur one another on towards
> love and good deeds. Let us not give up meeting together, as
> some are in the habit of doing, but let us encourage one
> another (Heb 10:24–25).

God is not asking us to lose our individuality, but our
independence. There is a great difference. Jesus appointed
the twelve disciples for the specific reason 'that they
might be with him' (Mk 3:14). He did not encourage a
'lone-ranger' ministry. Even when he wanted a donkey,
he sent two of his disciples to get it, two to prepare the
Passover supper. When he sent out the seventy fellows,

they were to go in pairs. In the early church it is noticeable that the apostles did not travel alone. Paul usually wrote in the plural as he was part of a team.

Interdependence was a hallmark of the early church as they continually submitted situations to one another, recognizing where God had delegated authority. The church today needs to invite the same spirit of submission to leadership if it is to be an effective voice in a world marked by a rebellious disregard for authority.

God gives great wisdom to those to whom he gives the responsibility of leadership, at every level of the body of Christ. Deuteronomy 34:9 says:

> Joshua was filled with the spirit of wisdom, because Moses had laid his hands on him.

God gave Joshua a special wisdom that equipped him for the task.

However, it would be foolish to think that all decisions made by leaders are automatically righteous. Although David was a good king he made some stupid choices which must have placed his senior men in great turmoil. For instance, David rejected the grave concern of his senior officer Joab and ordered him to number the people, which he reluctantly did. However, he refused to number the tribes of Levi and Benjamin because it was too abhorrent to him. What a dilemma for poor Joab! Some will say he should have disobeyed. In fact he did both; he obeyed by counting some, he disobeyed by not numbering all. His heart was divided. The question must be faced: is there a time to disobey? The answer must unequivocally be 'yes'! However, such a decision must always be carried out in a spirit of submission.

I am persuaded that such exceptions, although we must not disregard them, are not the major problem. We need to learn to trust God's delegated leadership in the body.

All that he is going to accomplish in the earth is to be through that body, so there is no place for those living independent lives. We need to be knit together. Submission to authority allows the body to work together in strength and unity.

6

Symptoms of Rebellion: Overwork and Weariness

Here is an extract from a letter that came from a man in India who received the tapes of our services.

Life has been very busy with our term in full swing here in the school, many responsibilities having piled up on us. Added to this, I have been operating out of the storeroom, having no laboratory as yet, as the materials have not come in time.

Jeremy, our younger boy took hepatitis three weeks ago. Nicky, our older boy, began vomiting uncontrollably one week ago, he too had hepatitis. Then last weekend I had to go to Delhi and back, 300 miles there and 300 miles back, in the heat of India, with bullock carts, rickshaws, cows and buffaloes to be avoided. Yesterday I almost collapsed at school and came home to bed. Was this the dreaded hepatitis? So I lay down and for the first time in about seven days I relaxed and fell asleep.

Then today, in bed, I started listening to you and to the second tape on rebellion. Well, brother, your treatment on the third category 'Doing good things God never wanted us to do' was so direct to me. Even Nicky, who was sitting up in bed with me, began to rejoice as well, knowing the pressure I had been under over the past weeks. But, praise the Lord, Barney, it was not a message to depress, but it shed the light of God on my present situation, a message leading to faith. Yes, I had become exhausted, busy with good things, but not God's will.

The wife of a home-cell leader told me she had come to the end of her resources. She said, 'I have run out of love for someone in our group.'

I said, 'Good!'

She looked at me and then continued speaking about the pressure, as though I had not spoken.

'I really can't go on,' were her next words.

I said, 'Praise the Lord.'

Startled, she asked, 'What do you mean by that?'

'God is bringing you to the end of your own resources.'

Her feeling was an example of what it means to be 'weary and heavy laden.' This is not the natural tiredness that comes after a day's hard work. There is a different weariness that comes when we are 'trying' to do something God has not given us the grace for. He uses that weariness to cause us to examine what we are doing when perhaps he wants us to stop.

Let me make three major comments about this kind of weariness:

1. At the heart of it is pride

At the heart of this kind of weariness is a pride that drives a person to make a good impression to earn the praise of men. 'I'll see this through even if it kills me,' people say—and it sometimes does. It brings on premature heart attacks, ulcers and all sorts of affliction, even cancer.

2. Possessiveness, also, is behind this weariness

It has to do with building our own little kingdom. We used to pray, 'Lord, bless this little corner of your vineyard.' God has a huge vineyard. There are no 'little corners' just for you and me, for our possession; rather, we are a people for his possession. It is God's kingdom and his work. A possessive person finds it difficult to delegate, for he cannot entrust tasks to others. He tends to be a perfectionist who is unwilling to risk the mistakes of others.

3. Independence results in weariness

Come to me, all you who are weary and burdened, and I will give you rest. Take my yoke upon you and learn from me, for I am gentle and humble in heart, and you will find rest for your souls. For my yoke is easy and my burden is light (Mt 11:28–30).

A yoke is a block of wood laid across the necks of two oxen so that one cannot go anywhere without the other while they remain joined by this yoke. They work and walk together. For Jesus to say 'come to me' indicates that he was appealing to people who had not submitted to be joined. A person who is not joined properly to Jesus becomes weary and burdened.

Have you ever been in a three-legged race? You can run providing the two of you move together. But if you take a step which your partner is not taking, you both tumble over. It can be painful!

Some people, even when they eventually put their neck in the yoke, do so reluctantly. They say, 'Yes, Lord, I want to be yoked. I want to be rid of all this rebellion.' But they do not realize what it is going to cost them. To be yoked with Jesus means that you walk with him, and you do what he is doing. When he does not go, you do not go. When he goes, you go. You had better go, because it is painful if you do not. It is the unbroken person who feels the pain of resisting the yoke.

A horse is a good example. Every untrained horse must reach a stage where it must be broken in if it is going to pull a cart or be ridden. There are men trained to do this breaking in. They get on that horse, and stay there until it begins to do what they want it to do. The horse may buck and veer frantically trying to throw off the rider. Finally, it is as though it says, 'OK I give in,' and it begins to walk and do whatever its rider indicates. It has been broken in. Some horses, however, can never properly be broken in. They remain rebels, wild and comparatively useless, for the rest of their lives.

So it is with many of God's people. They are strong, self-willed people, doing their own thing. They might even genuinely believe that what they are doing is good. But God did not initiate it. Such people will not flow with the rest of God's people. For example, when an important meeting is called, to which all others will be going, they can always find something more important that God wants them to do. They are even able to get a 'word from the Lord' to do it. Paul saw that there were certain elders at Ephesus who were acting independently and who would draw others after them. It caused him to weep (Acts 20:30–31). These were unbroken, self-willed leaders.

Bob Mumford uses the illustration about stroking a cat. If the cat is facing the wrong way then each stroke is unpleasant. All the cat has to do is turn around the other way and he can enjoy being stroked. The hand of the cat lover is a picture of God's hand. His whole heart is to reach out his hand and bless us bountifully, but if we are facing the wrong way, it is painful.

Our relationship with God is never negotiable. It is on God's terms alone. Jesus said in effect: 'If you want to know real rest and serenity, get yoked to me.' One of the most lovely things about Jesus is that he is very patient. At first, the yoke may bite into your neck because you are not moving at the same pace or time as the leader, Jesus. But as you learn to move in time and keep pace with the Lord, the abrasion disappears. Not being yoked to Jesus brings weariness and causes a person to be overloaded. It is a symptom of rebellion.

There are two ways of living as a child of God. One way

is by the flesh and the other is by the Spirit. Trying to make situations work by our own strength is called 'the arm of the flesh' (2 Chron 32:8). This brings weariness even to the routine tasks of life. Everything becomes a burden: being a father, a husband, at work and in the church.

I believe God actually allows the enemy to put burdens on us until we cannot cope. This may entail pain and great difficulties but when we cry for help, he is there immediately. He will often, in his mercy, bring us to the end of our own efforts quickly.

Sometimes he uses pressure from our children. Sometimes he may use our wives and then we wrongly see her as the source of our problem. She may be just an instrument that God uses to change us. When we recognize that God is speaking to us through the situation, and change, then she too will change.

The other way of living is by the Spirit. This is God's way for his children as we work with him, allowing him to lead and direct our ways.

> Brothers, I could not address you as spiritual but as worldly— mere infants in Christ.... You are still worldly. For since there is jealousy and quarrelling among you, are you not worldly? Are you not acting like mere men? (1 Cor 3:1, 3).

> By the grace God has given me, I laid a foundation as an expert builder, and someone else is building on it. But each one should be careful how he builds. For no-one can lay any foundation other than the one already laid, which is Jesus Christ. If any man builds on this foundation using gold, silver, costly stones, wood, hay or straw, his work will be shown for what it is, because the Day will bring it to light. It will be revealed with fire, and the fire will test the quality of each man's work. If what he has built survives, he will receive his reward. If it is burned up, he will suffer loss; he himself will be saved, but only as one escaping through the flames (1 Cor 3:10–15).

So here are the two ways of walking with God and doing the work of God. One is described as wood, hay and stubble. The other as gold, silver and precious stones. The former are my efforts, my strength, my will. The latter are his effort, his work, his strength and his way.

Let's now look at four areas where we can see these principles operating. In each of them we are faced with the choice between relying on our own strength, 'the arm of the flesh' or trusting and walking in the Spirit.

Marriage

Wives often take on the task of changing their husbands. A wife may do that in subtle ways with a word of encouragement here and there, or resort to persistent, nagging remonstrations. But is that her job? The Holy Spirit (in Ephesians 5) likens the marriage relationship to that of Jesus and the church. Who is the one who does the changing? It is Jesus who changes the church. It is obviously true that Jesus is perfect, unlike husbands, but the biblical challenge to wives is that they are primarily to submit to their husbands 'as to the Lord.' It is not for us to try and change the mind of the Lord or instruct him (1 Cor 2:16). It is for him to instruct us. Wives, it is for you to receive instruction from your husbands.

Some may say, 'But my husband is not a Christian.' Even in that situation, where it is possible, submit, other than in realms of sin. God still wants you to be submissive. Listen to these specific words in 1 Peter 3:1–2:

> Wives, in the same way be submissive to your husbands so that, if any of them do not believe the word, they may be won over without talk by the behaviour of their wives, when they see the purity and reverence of your lives.

Some have deep hurts in their marriage, which should not be under-rated. But we cannot bend the word of God to suit people's hurts and wounds. I would rather encourage people to find that the Lord is the One who binds up broken hearts, heals and restores.

Put your expectations in God to change your husband. I will give a simple example from my own married life. Some years ago we had a bad leak in the roof of our house and water was coming through the bedroom ceiling. It had become a real problem and was causing a good deal of stress, especially to my wife, Janette. Late that night as we prayed together I fell asleep while Janette was praying and did not hear her plea to the Lord to send someone along to repair the roof.

The next morning I said to Janette at breakfast time, 'Do you know what I think I will do, darling? If I borrowed the neighbour's step ladder, and got a broom handle and tied a brush to its end (I hate roofs!) I could dip it in some bitumen and lean over and paint it with a long arm.'

Janette said, 'Were you awake when I was praying last night?' I had to admit that I was not.

'Well,' she said, 'I prayed about that roof and asked the Lord to send someone along to do it.'

She had put her expectations in God, instead of nagging me, and I awoke that morning with a willing heart to do it. The scripture says it is God who is working in me both to will and to do his good pleasure—not my wife who is working on me to do her good pleasure. When we cast our burdens on the Lord, he undertakes to deal with them.

So wives need to release their husbands into God's hand and then watch him work out situations which may previously have caused so much frustration.

Children

We sometimes put great pressure on our children to behave well, especially if we are in the company of others and wish to impress them. It is not a desire to glorify the

Lord but has to do with pride. When we have visitors the most exhausting stress can be our concern about the children misbehaving. As often happens, that which we fear most comes upon us.

I remember when our boys were very small and we happened to have a well-known godly preacher coming to speak in our Sunday services; he was to stay in our home for the weekend. He was a rather quaint gentleman, somewhat Victorian, not given to light conversation. Unfortunately I was unable to be at home to welcome him and wasn't returning until after the Saturday evening meal. My wife became very anxious; she had met him previously, and done all she could to impress strongly upon the boys that they must behave themselves. For instance she said, 'Don't slurp when you drink your tea.' Unfortunately the first thing our respectable guest did when he took his cup of tea was to slurp! My two sons burst out laughing—and Mum couldn't help laughing too!

Then to her horror one of them, now inspired by the new atmosphere of merriment, proceeded to tell a joke about three black men falling over a cliff. Needless to say, it was in terribly poor taste and Janette was very embarrassed. She kept glaring at the culprit, but to no avail. He cheerfully completed his story. Our preacher, meanwhile, was not amused and treated the whole incident with obvious disdain. Like Job of old, Janette could say, 'The thing which I greatly feared is come upon me.'

It is wrong to get burdened with worry about how your children are going to behave with guests, particularly if it is the pastor who is visiting. Why do we play this silly game and pressurize our children to act differently from normal because we have visitors? If it is pride that causes us to feel such pressure, then God will ensure that the little darlings do it all wrong! God can 'oppose the proud' (Jas 4:6) even through our children.

Like most people, I enjoy hearing favourable comments

about my children and their behaviour. But I had to come to a place of peace so that I could accept the way they were. If they did misbehave, that peace prevented me from dealing harshly with the children in front of others, if that was not the appropriate time to speak to them.

We need to trust God, too, with our children and realize he is alongside us in our care for them. We should not give in to the pressure of 'what will people think?' Obviously the answer is consistent loving discipline, visitors or not.

The church

The psalmist says, 'Unless the Lord builds the house, its builders labour in vain' (Ps 127:1). This is so important to all missionaries and church leaders. Unless God is totally directing what we are doing we are wasting our time. Everything we do out of our own efforts and ideas is only wood, hay and stubble. Sadly there is a spirit of Babel in the church of Jesus Christ, and it is this: 'Let us make a name for ourselves' (Gen 11:4). God will blow upon it and it will all tumble down. He will not share his glory with any man, and eventually it will collapse like a pack of cards.

We once had the Principal of the Elim Bible College visiting our church. Deep inside, I wanted to make a good impression but somehow was not aware of it at the time. We were moving charismatically and on this Sunday morning I put pressure on the congregation to lift up their hands to the Lord. They dutifully put their hands up, but it wasn't 'born of the Spirit'; it was of the flesh. Graciously, they forgave me, but you cannot bulldoze, push or even prod people to change.

If the Spirit of God is not doing it, it will not happen. But that which is of the Spirit will happen and will remain. It will become part of the foundation of the building which only the Lord can build. Missionaries, evangelists, pastors, teachers, youth leaders, home-cell leaders need above all to wait upon God and get his directions. Then they can operate out of obedience. Being yoked to Jesus is the easy way and brings success.

The ministry

It is not *my* ministry, it is his. Paul, the great apostle and missionary, writes to the Corinthians:

> I came to you in weakness and fear, and with much trembling (1 Cor 2:3).

That is a good fear; it is part of the fear of the Lord. However he also added:

> My message and my preaching were not in persuasive words of wisdom, but in demonstration of the Spirit and of power (v.4 NASB).

For God to be strong it was necessary for Paul to be weak. In fact, we understand that God specifically made him weak. He had revelations and was caught up into the third heaven, but he said:

> To keep me from becoming conceited because of these surpassingly great revelations, there was given me a thorn in my flesh, a messenger of Satan, to torment me (2 Cor 12:7).

Many sermons discuss what Paul's 'thorn in the flesh' might be but, in fact, I don't think it is particularly important. The really important issue is a danger of pride in Paul because of his ministry. It is as though the devil encourages us, 'Teach and emphasize the thorn in the flesh but, whatever you do, don't emphasize what God is really saying there. People might realize their pride, humble themselves and be exalted by God for greater purposes.'

The danger is that pride in '*my* ministry' may lead me into too much performance and show. It may also cause me to take on many things God does not want me to do just because I feel I'm so important. God does not want you and me to be rushing here and there to minister. The key question is: 'What does *God* want?'

Paul learned through weakness to depend on God more fully.

> Three times I pleaded with the Lord to take it away from me. But he said to me, 'My grace is sufficient for you, for my power is made perfect in weakness.' Therefore I will boast all the more gladly about my weaknesses, so that Christ's power may rest on me (2 Cor 12:8–9).

God does not want a one-man ministry but the ministry of the One Man—our exalted Lord and Christ—operating through us.

An idol called 'ministry'

Before finishing this chapter, let me add one further point. Some men treat their ministry as if it were a god, sacrificing on its altar their wife, children, friends and eventually their own health. Their favourite motto is: 'I'd rather burn out than rust out.' They will protect 'the ministry' at all costs, even at the price of integrity. Sometimes they see their ministry as more important than the need for character adjustment. Instead of getting help when they fall into sin, they cover it, for fear that if they sought help they would be counselled to step down from the ministry. So every time they step into the pulpit to speak God's word to God's people a little voice whispers in their mind: 'You're not worthy... you hypocrite—how can you stand and deliver God's word knowing you are a secret sinner... How can you exhort other people to confess their sins while you retain your own dark secret?'

They either push out of their minds such condemning thoughts or the accusation drags them down into shame, depression and darkness. One such man, who confessed his sin of adultery to me, rushed to the bathroom and actually vomited, such was the intense emotion he experienced. There were floods of tears but such great relief! Although he laid down his ministry temporarily while his marriage was rebuilt, today he is engaged in a most fruitful ministry and enjoys a loving, guilt-free marriage.

> He who conceals his transgressions will not prosper, but he who confesses and forsakes them will find compassion (Prov 28:13 NASB).

> How blessed is the man to whom the Lord does not impute iniquity, and in whose spirit there is no deceit! When I kept silent about my sin my body wasted away (Ps 32:2–3 NASB).

> Confess your sins to one another (Jas 5:16 NASB).

One final word of caution. There is a right time to confess sin. Let God decide when that time is. You will find his timing is accompanied with an indescribable sense of peace. The issue is not whether to confess sin but *when*.

7

Symptoms of Rebellion: The Unbridled Tongue

The tongue is very powerful. It is only a small part of the body but its effect is devastating. It is like a match cast carelessly in the dry bracken of a forest. The fire that starts up can consume thousands of acres, property and even lives. Such, too, are the dangers of an unbridled tongue.

Make a tree good and its fruit will be good, or make a tree bad and its fruit will be bad, for a tree is recognised by its fruit. You brood of vipers, how can you who are evil say anything good? For out of the overflow of the heart the mouth speaks. The good man brings things out of the good stored up in him, and the evil man brings evil things out of the evil stored up in him. But I tell you that men will have to give account on the day of judgment for every careless word they have spoken. For by your words you will be acquitted, and by your words you will be condemned (Mt 12:33–37).

The tongue has the power of life and death (Prov 18:21).

The good man brings good things out of the good stored up in his heart, and the evil man brings evil things out of the evil stored up in his heart. For out of the overflow of his heart, his mouth speaks (Lk 6:45).

We can work hard at saying the right things and keep it

up for quite some time. But, finally, out of the abundance of our heart our mouth will speak. It will come out when our defences are down. Perhaps when someone close says something that annoys or hurts. Then the 'treasure' of our heart is poured out and perhaps it will surprise us.

We have already seen how rebellion lies in the subconscious mind. It is like bad breath: usually the person who has it does not know it. The Spirit of God wants to bring every vestige of rebellion to the surface so that it can be dealt with rather than leaving it there to be manifested in times of stress.

The day that we were born, deposited unceremoniously into the world, we began to reign as a little monarch. Hungry? Uncomfortable? We cried, our servants ran to our aid and we quickly learned how to gain an audience and have the attention of all present. In fact, it wasn't too long before we began playing mum against dad, or teacher against both of them. Now we are adults, but adults are only grown-up children and we still have strong inclinations to control.

But God did not make us to be the centre of the universe. The Lord Jesus is to be the centre, and only when he is King is there 'righteousness, peace and joy in the Holy Spirit' (Rom 14:17).

What fills our heart determines what comes out of our mouth. When rebellion is rooted out, the treasure of our heart becomes the Lord Jesus. His words are always gracious and true; his words then come out of our mouths.

The measure of real control we have on our tongues is the measure of the Lordship of Christ within us. If what comes out of our mouths reveals rebellion, Jesus is not really Lord. Reverencing Christ as Lord in my heart means a daily experiencing of Jesus being Lord. It does not mean just standing up in a gathering and declaring it on one or two occasions, but living in the good of his Lordship, hour by hour.

Not many of you should presume to be teachers, my brothers, because you know that we who teach will be judged more strictly. We all stumble in many ways. If anyone is never at fault in what he says, he is a perfect man, able to keep his whole body in check. When we put bits into the mouths of horses to make them obey us, we can turn the whole animal. Or take ships as an example. Although they are so large and are driven by strong winds, they are steered by a very small rudder wherever the pilot wants to go. Likewise the tongue is a small part of the body, but it makes great boasts. Consider what a great forest is set on fire by a small spark. The tongue also is a fire, a world of evil among the parts of the body. It corrupts the whole person, sets the whole course of his life on fire, and is itself set on fire by hell (Jas 3:1–6).

Jesus pointed out, 'What goes into a man's mouth does not make him "unclean", but what comes out of his mouth, that is what makes him "unclean".' As we read in James 3:6 (AV) the tongue 'setteth on fire the course of nature.'

Indeed, many of God's people are sick because of what comes out of their mouths. Their tongue sets on fire the cycle of nature, and their body does not function wholly the way God would have it. When we let out our thoughts, we are, as it were, signing and sealing those thoughts, having made a public confession of them.

All kinds of animals, birds, reptiles and creatures of the sea are being tamed and have been tamed by man, but no man can tame the tongue. It is a restless evil, full of deadly poison (Jas 3:7–8).

We cannot tame our tongue. It is only Jesus as Lord in our life who can do it.

Let us look at some of the aspects of the tongue that displease God.

The lying tongue

In Proverbs God talks of seven things which he hates. One of them is a lying tongue. Two major causes of a lying tongue are fear and hate.

Fear causes us to be defensive and self-protecting. It causes us to be deceived and to deceive others. We worry what might happen if we told the truth about a situation that reveals our sin or inadequacy.

When my daughter, Rachel, was three or four years old, I had taken her out in the car. I left her for a few minutes and when I returned she blurted out, her mouth stuffed with sweets, 'Daddy, I haven't touched your sweets.' I hadn't asked her about them, but she was fearful of what might happen to her if I discovered she had been eating them.

On another occasion I faced a fellow Christian with the fact that I knew he had told me a plain lie. For about fifteen minutes, he continued to make up stories, trying hard to justify himself. It was not until we prayed together that he broke down and told the truth. He was afraid of what might happen, as he held a position of responsibility and did not want to lose it.

Fear will keep an unfaithful husband or wife from telling the truth. Often I have counselled husbands or wives who have carried a burden of guilt for years. The only answer is to tell the truth. There is freedom in truth, but bondage in lying.

There is also a fear of rejection which causes us to deceive through exaggeration. Even ministers can be prone to this form of lying. An evangelist may say that 300 were present at a particular meeting, whereas 150 would be nearer the truth. He lies almost unconsciously because of the pressure for success that will bring acceptance by the church or society that is supporting him. Often this sort of person has a poor self-image.

A rebellious person finds it difficult to love himself. Hence the need to go beyond the truth to something sensational. Similarly a 'super-spiritual' person lacks self-love and drives himself on to appear more spiritual than he really is. This is borne out of inadequacy and can lead such people to pray in strange tones and in a religious language that is unreal for them.

The Lord has made us all unique and different, and he is not in the business of making mistakes. We need to accept ourselves as God made us and thank him for the way we are made. Otherwise we could be led into dangerous deception such as happened to Ananias and Sapphira (Acts 5). They told the apostles that they had sold a field and were giving, *oh yes,* the total amount to God. But in fact they brought only a portion of it. That is being super-spiritual. Peter said, 'How is it that Satan has so filled your heart that you have lied to the Holy Spirit?' Peter went on, 'While it remained unsold it was under your control. Even after selling it, you could have done what you liked with the money. You could have even given just a portion and kept some. But you said you had given all of it. So God is dealing with you.' Ananias dropped dead, as did his wife Sapphira later in the day, because she also adopted this super-spiritual pose with her husband.

Over the years I have seen many people who are constantly super-spiritual, or 'pseudo-spiritual' to give it a more precise title. Some people find it difficult to pray to their Father in heaven without adopting an unnatural stammering style. Others groan and sigh or inhale in strange ways.

God wants us to be ourselves and communicate with him in ways that truly express our hearts. This means that we can talk in our usual English and breathe normally.

For example, I remember hearing a young convert praying to the Lord, telling God he was 'just great!' I encouraged him to continue to have that kind of normal relationship. God wants us to be reverent but not unreal.

Hate is the other major cause of a lying tongue. When someone hurts us, we often desire to get our own back—this is the beginning of hate. Proverbs 10:12 declares that 'hatred stirs up dissension'—or strife.

> A malicious man disguises himself with his lips, but in his heart he harbours deceit. Though his speech is charming, do not believe him, for seven abominations fill his heart. His malice may be concealed by deception, but his wickedness will be exposed in the assembly.
>
> If a man digs a pit, he will fall into it; if a man rolls a stone, it will roll back on him.
>
> A lying tongue hates those it hurts, and a flattering mouth works ruin (Prov 26:24–28).

A person who is prone to lying very often bears resentment and bitterness in his heart. It could be towards someone in the family, or a teacher, a boss at work, or a neighbour. Perhaps something painful was said and it's never been cleared. It is not always obvious that a person holds hate in his heart. He learns to disguise it, but a lying tongue reveals his inner struggle.

The gossiping tongue

In the list of seven things that God hates, the thing that God detests the most vehemently is he 'who stirs up dissension among brothers':

> He who covers over an offence promotes love, but whoever repeats the matter separates close friends (Prov 17:9).

Gossiping is repeating a matter. It is helpful when in doubt about repeating a matter to ask oneself the following three questions:

Is it kind?
Is it true?
Is it necessary?

Gossiping uncovers another person. Proverbs describes it as being like choice morsels that 'go down to a man's inmost parts' (Prov 18:8). The misuse of the tongue in this way probably causes more problems in a family, or community of God's people, than anything else.

A pastor once visited one of his congregation who was a gossiper. He took a newspaper and said to the lady, 'I would like you to tear up the newspaper into tiny shreds and then go around the town throwing the pieces everywhere. Then a few hours later, pick up all the bits and put them back together.'

'Oh, I couldn't do that. The wind will have blown them away.'

'Exactly,' he said. 'It's like that when you gossip, you can never take it back. Once out, it will go wherever people will take it and usually it gets embellished and enlarged.'

I remember a time when a rumour circulated that I had 'joined the jetset' as a preacher. I was leading the praise and worship at a major conference in England. The story was that someone had died in Vancouver, Canada and that I had immediately caught a plane and returned to take the funeral. The truth was that my father who lived in southern England died and I simply left the England conference to attend his funeral. No doubt the gossip who began the rumour was not aware of all the facts but the 'jetset' story spread quickly.

Another time, back in England, we had begun to dance before the Lord, as David had in Old Testament times. A story began to circulate that I was giving dancing lessons at the church. What actually happened was that we were doing a musical which required some dance and drama, and a lady was giving some help to the actors, teaching them to dance gracefully. But these lessons were not given by me! Later the tale became embellished to include the fact that Barney was giving dancing lessons, so that when he danced in the Spirit, all would dance the same way. (Actually there is no such thing as dancing in the Spirit.)

Gossip is perhaps an area that older women are particularly vulnerable to. In Titus 2:3 we read:

> Likewise, teach the older women to be reverent in the way they live, not to be slanderers ['malicious gossips' NASB].

> Gossiping tongues cause contention: Without wood a fire goes out; without gossip a quarrel dies down (Prov 26:20).

Finally, what is one to do when someone comes with gossip? An answer is given in Proverbs 20:19: 'A gossip betrays confidence, so avoid a man who talks too much.' If you don't associate with them, they have no one with whom to gossip.

Paul told Timothy that malicious gossiping is a sign of the end times:

> In the last days...men will be...malicious gossips (2 Tim 3:1–3 NASB).

Rumour-mongering will increase, and if we are going to be a light in a dark world, we must deal with it radically in ourselves by the grace of the Lord Jesus. Bring it to him and say, 'Jesus, this thing is bigger than I can handle. I find myself gossiping so much. Please, Lord Jesus, reign over me and root it out.'

The grumbling tongue

God's anger is ignited by grumbling. We read in Numbers 11:1:

> Now the people complained about their hardships in the hearing of the Lord, and when he heard them, his anger was aroused.

Grumbling and complaining are ultimately against God. It may *seem* as if it is against your husband, wife, children, pastors, elders, but it is ultimately against God because his command is: 'In everything give thanks' (see 1 Thess 5:18 and Col 3:17). Grumbling is saying, in effect, 'God, you've made a mistake. I don't approve of what you're doing.'

God hates grumbling that is directed towards his anointed leaders. This is very relevant because leaders are continually the object of grumbling. This has always been so, but God's attitude to it has never changed.

Here is dramatic illustration from Numbers 12:

> Miriam and Aaron began to talk against Moses because of his Cushite wife, for he had married a Cushite. 'Has the Lord spoken only through Moses?' they asked. 'Hasn't he also spoken through us?' and the Lord heard this. (Now Moses was a very humble man, more humble than anyone else on the face of the earth.) At once the Lord said to Moses, Aaron and Miriam, 'Come out to the Tent of Meeting, all three of you.' So the three of them came out. Then the Lord came down in a pillar of cloud; he stood at the entrance to the Tent and summoned Aaron and Miriam. When both of them stepped forward, he said, 'Listen to my words: "When a prophet of the Lord is among you, I reveal myself to him in visions, I speak to him in dreams. But this is not true of my servant Moses; he is faithful in all my house. With him I speak face to face, clearly and not in riddles; he sees the form of the Lord. Why then were you not afraid to speak against my servant Moses?"' (vv. 1–8).

God's anger was unleashed upon Miriam and Aaron to the extent that they had to return to Moses to plead with him to pray for them. When he did so, Miriam was healed of her leprosy. God put them in a place where they needed the very leader about whom they had complained so that he could bring about a change in their rebellious attitude.

Of course no leader has the right to enforce his authority for his authority comes from God. God leads us to a place where we can make the right decisions but never forces those decisions upon us. Frequently, however, he will use circumstances to demonstrate how effective the ministry of a delegated authority can be.

One of my elders relates that he was seeking for baptism in the Holy Spirit, but wasn't getting anywhere. He began to realize that he wasn't accepting me as his leader at that time. There came a point when God said to him, 'The only way you will receive this baptism is for you to go to Barney, ask him to lay hands on you and pray, and submit to his authority.' The day he did that, he was baptized in the Spirit. That was not because I have some special talent in that direction. It is because God stands by those he has anointed to be leaders though he does this in a variety of ways. He will focus on those areas of weakness in your family situation, your marriage, or your work and take his hand of protection away until you reach the kind of problem that will push you to seek help. When you do it God's way, it works.

The grumbling tongue is a symptom of rebellion. 'Do everything without complaining or arguing' says the Holy Spirit through Paul in Philippians 2:14. Peter writes: 'Offer hospitality to one another without grumbling' (1 Pet 4:9). Be careful of such comments as, 'Did you notice she didn't lift a finger to help me in the kitchen!' Does that ring a bell with any wives reading this? Or, 'He could at least have taken his shoes off, coming in out of that heavy rain!' All right, he should have. But we're not to complain. We are to be 'hospitable without grumbling.'

The contentious tongue

Here are some verses that speak about the contentious or quarrelsome tongue:

> A foolish son is his father's ruin, and a quarrelsome wife is like a constant dripping (Prov 19:13).

> Better to live on a corner of the roof than share a house with a quarrelsome wife (Prov 21:9).

> Better to live in a desert than with a quarrelsome and ill-tempered wife (Prov 21:19).

> As charcoal to embers and as wood to fire, so is a quarrelsome man for kindling strife (Prov 26:21).

In Scripture, contention is directly linked with rebellion. The argumentative, quarrelsome complaints of Korah in Numbers 16 are quite clearly branded as rebellion: 'the rebellion of Korah' (Jude 11).

> Korah son of Izhar, the son of Kohath, the son of Levi, and certain Reubenites—Dathan and Abiram, sons of Eliab, and On son of Peleth—became insolent and rose up against Moses. With them were 250 Israelite men, well-known community leaders who had been appointed members of the council. They came as a group to oppose Moses and Aaron and said to them, 'You have gone too far! The whole community is holy, every one of them, and the Lord is with them. Why then do you set yourselves above the Lord's assembly?' When Moses heard this, he fell face down. Then he said to Korah and all his followers: 'In the morning the Lord will show who belongs to him and who is holy, and he will make that person come near him. The man he chooses he will cause to come near him' (Num 16:1–5).

At the end of this story the earth opened up and swallowed the sons of Korah and their households and even the men who belonged to Korah, with all their possessions.

What are we to do with factious, contentious, divisive people? An answer is found in Titus 3:10:

> Warn a divisive person once, then warn him a second time. After that, have nothing to do with him.

Be honest with them, but if there is no response, withdraw from fellowship with them, then leave it to God to deal with them.

Blessings of the tongue

What we have looked at perhaps seems rather heavy but there is much emphasis in Scripture on these kinds of tongues and God's serious attitude towards them. However, it is good to see that although they may be destructive, tongues can bless in powerful ways too:

> A gentle answer turns away wrath, but a harsh word stirs up anger (Prov 15:1).

> Reckless words pierce like a sword, but the tongue of the wise brings healing (Prov 12:18).

> A soothing tongue is a tree of life (Prov 15:4 NASB).

> The wise in heart are called discerning, and pleasant words promote instruction (Prov 16:21).

> Pleasant words are a honeycomb, sweet to the soul and healing to the bones (Prov 16:24).

> Let your conversation be always full of grace, seasoned with salt, so that you may know how to answer everyone (Col 4:6).

Words from our mouths can soothe and heal in a beautiful way. What we say can actually affect people in their bodies as well as spiritually and emotionally.

Jesus said, 'The words I have spoken to you are spirit, and they are life' (Jn 6:63). He also said, 'As the Father has sent me, I am sending you' (Jn 20:21). In other words, Jesus is sending us so we will be those whose words to others are spirit and life. We hold in our tongue the power of life and death, healing or destruction, health or sickness.

God wants us to be constantly ministering life, constantly thankful, constantly appreciative to people, encouraging, strengthening and uplifting them. Words are a tremendous force for good! It was with a word that God created the heavens and the earth. Either God uses our words or the devil uses them. There is no middle course. We are accountable for every word that comes out of our mouths. A sobering thought!

8

Symptoms of Rebellion: Imbalance

Another word for *imbalance* is *eccentric*, which means 'off centre'. Where there is submission in the spirit of a person there is perfect balance, for Jesus is enthroned in the centre of that life. Imbalance is a symptom of rebellion, demonstrating that Jesus is not totally Lord.

Our personalities are all quite different and God rejoices in that variety of expression he gave to man, his creation. Nevertheless, he created us in his image, to display his beauty and form. He is a God of order and is complete. The work of the Spirit in our lives is to enable us to change from our fallen, rebellious, eccentric selves to being balanced and beautiful. Otherwise, our peculiarities, borne out of rebellion, serve to repulse the unbeliever as he judges God on what he sees in us, God's ambassadors.

On one occasion at Heathrow Airport I saw this in operation, damaging the work of God in a new believer. I was accompanied by two men, an American friend and a Canadian I had just met. During a delay at the airport the American found a lost wallet in a telephone booth. We suggested he handed it in at the information desk.

Now this man was always ready for any opportunity that the Spirit might lead him to share Jesus with others.

So, after looking at the photograph in the wallet, he went off in the direction of the desk, slipping a little pamphlet into it on the way. Fifteen minutes later, he returned, accompanied by a beaming Nigerian and introduced him. 'Meet my new brother in the Lord!' He had recognized him from the photo while on the way to the desk! While returning the wallet to him, my American friend explained how he had slipped in the leaflet and gone straight on to share the Lord Jesus with him.

The Nigerian was amazed and said, 'So many people in the last few days have been speaking to me about Jesus. It seems that God is out to get me, and I'm giving in!' So right there, in that bustling airport lounge, he gave over his heart and life to Jesus Christ.

It was then that the Canadian came along. On hearing the story, far from sharing the Nigerian's new-found joy and encouraging him, he began to probe him aggressively, trying to ensure that he really was born again. 'If you were to walk out of this building and get killed by a car, would you go to heaven or hell?' He pressed him even further, tritely using evangelical jargon to attack the new believer. By speaking the way he did, he reduced the sensitive dealings of God in the Nigerian's life to a 'ticket to heaven'. Apart from the confusion he caused, the Canadian's attitude presented an imbalanced picture of what a Christian is, with no emphasis on the Lordship of Christ or explanation about being a disciple.

Being 'balanced' can be compared to a pair of scissors —both blades are needed to produce a cutting edge. In Scripture, truth seems to be held in tension. Frequently, God puts two truths alongside each other and each brings a balance to the other. One truth over-emphasized at the expense of the other can become a heresy. Here are some important examples:

Balance: rhema and logos

Both the Greek words *rhema* and *logos* are translated *word* in English.

> But what does it say? 'The word is near you; it is in your mouth and in your heart,' that is, the word of faith we are proclaiming: That if you confess with your mouth, 'Jesus is Lord,' and believe in your heart that God raised him from the dead, you will be saved. For it is with your heart that you believe and are justified, and it is with your mouth that you confess and are saved. As the Scripture says, 'Everyone who trusts in him will never be put to shame.' For there is no difference between Jew and Gentile—the same Lord is Lord of all and richly blesses all who call on him, for, 'Everyone who calls on the name of the Lord will be saved.'
>
> How then, can they call on the one they have not believed in? And how can they believe in the one of whom they have not heard? And how can they hear without someone preaching to them? And how can they preach unless they are sent? As it is written, 'How beautiful are the feet of those who bring good news!'
>
> But not all the Israelites accepted the good news. For Isaiah says: 'Lord, who has believed our message?' Consequently, faith comes from hearing the message, and the message is heard through the word of Christ (Rom 10:8–17).

Rhema is an inspired utterance for the occasion, and it requires action; it normally inspires faith in a person to do what God wants him to do. For example, the young maiden, Mary, listened to the angel telling her of the forthcoming birth of Jesus, and she responded with 'May it be to me as you have said' (Lk 1:38).

Peter fished all night with his fellow disciples, and caught nothing. When Jesus told him to let down his net on the other side of the boat, he said:

Master, we have toiled all night and have taken nothing:
nevertheless at thy word [rhema] I will let down the net (Lk
5:5 AV).

When we are praying for healing, it is crucial that we
have a word, a *rhema* for a healing. That is why James
says: 'The prayer offered in faith will make the sick person
well.' In the original this is simply 'the prayer of faith'. 'So
faith comes from hearing and hearing by the word of
Christ' (Rom 10:17 NASB), in the Greek, a *rhema* of
Christ.

When God speaks a 'now' word, a *rhema* into our
hearts concerning, for instance, health, it is important to
believe and move on this faith word from Christ. God
watches over his *rhema*, his 'now word', his 'faith word' to
perform it.

The *logos*, on the other hand, is the unchanging eternal
truth and revelation of God. It is objective, unchanging
and abiding. We as God's people need to read and medi-
tate on the Scriptures, the *logos* of God, so that it is
indelibly imprinted on our subconscious minds. It then
becomes a measuring rod within us and a way of life.

The ultimate expression of the *logos* was Jesus Christ,
'the same yesterday, today and for ever.' God wants us to
know this unchanging One, God's Logos, not for what he
does, primarily, but for what he is. The *rhema* has to do
with what he does; the *logos* has to do with what he is.

Let us bring all this down to practical daily living. Just
after you have been born again or baptized in the Holy
Spirit, Jesus is unutterably real. He appears to be speaking
to you out of everything around you and each circum-
stance. God does speak to specific situations through
Scripture verses—and the *logos* becomes a *rhema* to us.
God called me out of my job as a London policeman with
such a word, and I would not belittle it. But nevertheless it
can be dangerous, an imbalance, when a person lives all

day and every day in the *rhema* especially if that *rhema* contradicts the *logos*.

Here is a rather extreme illustration. When filling in an income-tax return, one could say, 'Well, I don't see that I should pay this. Lord, should I pay this? Give me a special word.' So the Bible is opened at that day's reading. 'Ah! Here it is! "To you the riches of the nations shall come."' So the erroneous conclusion is drawn: 'That must mean tax gatherers. Well, I won't declare it all. God has given his word.' No, he hasn't! God never gives a *rhema* that contradicts his *logos*, and his *logos* is very clear in Scripture, 'Pay your taxes.' It's a command in Matthew 22:21: 'Give to Caesar what is Caesar's, and to God what is God's.'

Here's an example from a church in which I was involved. A pastor and the wife of another pastor were having an unholy relationship together. One day, the woman said to a friend 'Look, if my husband telephones, tell him I've just left.'

'Isn't that telling a lie?' said the friend.

'Ah, in Eastern Europe, Christians behind the Iron Curtain have to tell lies sometimes to preserve their lives, and to preserve the life we have in Jesus, we have to tell lies sometimes. It is right.'

Where did such wrong thinking begin?

It was the fruit of a root which had begun when another couple in this church had wanted to get married. The man had been newly divorced in order that he could remarry. When the church leaders met to discuss the situation, this particular pastor's wife had said, 'Well, I don't see it in the word (*logos*) but I *feel* God is saying it's all right.'

By operating on this lady's feelings, the *logos* was contradicted, paving the way for further deception in her own life. I repeat, the *rhema* will never contradict the *logos*.

When a young person comes to me and says, 'I want to marry this person—a non-Christian; God has told me to do so,' I know he or she is deceived. God's *logos* says clearly: 'Do not be yoked together with unbelievers.' That's the unchanging word of God.

We charismatics are very susceptible to this kind of deception. We begin to live in the *rhema* and say, 'Oh, praise God, he speaks today. I've heard his voice.' Of course he speaks and we can hear—but he never speaks to break his own word. He is the unchanging God.

Here is the principle: the *rhema* must *always* be subject to the *logos*. It is no good saying, 'Jesus told me' or, 'I've had a vision or a dream' if what we have heard or seen does not fit into the eternal *logos*. On the other hand, the *logos* without the *rhema* also produces an imbalance. It can become a cold, orthodox, lifeless religion. It can even produce unbelief, which God abhors, for unbelief, too, is rebellion. The *rhema* and the *logos* in balance with each other as God's word in us, bring about solid, living, life-changing growth.

Balance: law and grace

Will you not revive us again, that your people may rejoice in you?

Show us your unfailing love, O Lord, and grant us your salvation.

I will listen to what God the Lord will say; he promises peace to his people, his saints—but let them not return to folly.

Surely his salvation is near those who fear him, that his glory may dwell in our land.

Love and faithfulness meet together; righteousness and peace kiss each other.

Faithfulness springs forth from the earth, and righteousness looks down from heaven.

The Lord will indeed give what is good and our land will yield its harvest.

Righteousness goes before him and prepares the way for his steps (Ps 85:6–13).

Here we see another balance: righteousness and peace kiss each other. As John 1:17 says: 'The law was given through Moses; grace and truth came through Jesus Christ.'

The law, 'Thou shalt not,' was given by Moses. Grace *and* 'thou shalt not' came through Jesus Christ. Grace without truth is shallow and can lead, as I have often seen, to permissiveness.

The Christians at Rome received a revelation of grace, so they thought. 'Well, the grace of God is so phenomenal, we want to give God every opportunity to express it. So the more we sin, the more he can forgive us, and the more it proves his grace.'

So Paul had to write to them, 'You've got it all wrong. Sin must not continue that grace may abound.' God wants grace and truth to be held in a beautiful balance. Grace without truth makes us become presumptuous regarding God's mercy. Truth without grace leads to bigotry, bitterness and resentment. As Paul wrote elsewhere: 'The letter kills, but the Spirit gives life' (2 Cor 3:6). God never intended that it was one against or instead of the other. Grace and truth have 'kissed' each other in Jesus Christ.

Some say that since Jesus came we are in the New Covenant. Laws have to do with the Old Covenant. And you may even be thinking as you read these pages: 'Aren't you getting a bit legalistic, keeping on about rebellion and independence?'

I find that those who genuinely desire to do the will of God find it life-giving and releasing to walk within the divine lines drawn for them. If you are rebelling at all, it will be difficult, for the discipline of the Lord is painful. Later on, however, 'it produces a harvest of righteousness and peace for those who have been trained by it' (Heb 12:11).

Jesus said in John 13:34, 'A new commandment I give you: Love one another. As I have loved you, so you must love one another.' It would be wrong to take that verse and infer that all other commands are cancelled. Jesus took the old commandment, 'Love your neighbour as yourself' and added to it. How do I love myself? I look after myself, feed and clothe myself. That's all very good. But Jesus was saying: 'I am giving you a *new* commandment. You are, from now on, to love one another *as you have seen me love you*. He did not cancel all the other commandments, in fact, he added some. That is why in his final commission to his disciples, he said, 'Therefore go and make disciples of all nations...teaching them to obey *everything I have commanded you*' (Mt 28:19–20).

The commandments of God did not end when Jesus came: indeed, for the first time ever, a man kept the law and fulfilled it. He clarified what was God's heart in the law. For example he said, 'You have heard that it was said, "Do not commit adultery." But I tell you that anyone who looks at a woman lustfully has already committed adultery with her in his heart (Mt 5:27–28). He changed the emphasis from the action alone to include what was within a man.

God, we are told, requires 'truth in the inner parts' (Ps 51:6). The outward without the inward is legalism. But if the outward observance flows from inner conviction and integrity, it is the law of the Spirit of life in Christ Jesus, which 'sets me free from the law of sin and death' (Rom 8:2). Not my striving and struggling, but Christ living and working in me to cause me to act according to his good purpose (Phil 2:13).

We need to pray each morning, 'Lord, I want to do your will today. Help me to do it.' And this should not be a burden. We can relax in God who has said: 'I will put my laws into their minds and write them upon their hearts.'

So the Old Testament commandments, for example, 'You shall not steal' (Ex 20:15) meaning 'You *must* not steal,' becomes in the New Testament context, a promise and a declaration that as Christians we *shall* not steal. We become more than conquerors through him who loves us—not by human endeavour but by God's Spirit.

The New Testament is full of words of command and we do need them. But with each command is the grace, power, ability and life of Jesus to do God's will and give him pleasure.

Balance: horizontal and vertical relationships

People who emphasize only the vertical relationship, that is, 'just Jesus and me', usually react unfavourably to the people who talk about the need for horizontal relationships with each other. But we need both: the vertical and the horizontal.

The vertical without the horizontal fellowship will engender deception. This sort of independent person constantly says, 'The Lord said to me....' and if you disagree, that makes *you* 'unspiritual'.

One man told a Christian brother, 'The Lord told me you are to give me $500.' The brother replied, 'Well, it's strange, but God hasn't told me that.' That is one appropriate reply!

One writer said, 'If I hear the voice of God so clearly that I do not need my brother or sister to adjust it or add to it, then I have become a little pope.' Many evangelicals point their finger at the Pope but themselves are little popes because they say they hear from God in an exclusively vertical way. They do not allow brothers and sisters to bring adjustment to their lives. They are afraid that someone might say, for example, 'We believe that it is time you stayed at home more, and looked after your children a little more.' We are 'members one of another', bond-slaves of Christ with no rights of our own.

There is freedom within the bondage of Jesus. There is freedom when the horizontal relationship is held in balance with the vertical. The horizontal produces naturalness and fun. That is the good side of it, but on its own it will eventually produce unedifying conversation, worldliness, foolish jesting and prayerlessness.

The vertical without the horizontal produces super-spirituality, which is a form of deception, makes a person unteachable, as they become a law unto themselves. But when there is a good relationship with the Lord, and a loving relationship with our brothers and sisters, we have a balanced Christian walk.

The Scriptures do not record, 'I have the mind of Christ.' It's '*we* have the mind of Christ', in plurality. We all need the body of Christ, because it is a God-provided check on eccentricities and excesses. When I was a boy we used to do sums where adding, either vertically or horizontally, produced the same answer. They were called logarithms. It is the same in the Christian life. We must be checked vertically and horizontally. This gives security in God.

Balance: The gifts and fruit of the Spirit

Here is another area where we see extremes of views that confuse the work of the Spirit. Some stress the importance of the operation of the gifts of the Spirit such as tongues, interpretation of tongues, healing and prophecy. Others refuse to accept such gifts and stress the importance of the fruit of the Spirit such as love, joy and peace. They point to 1 Corinthians 13 and say love is the most important of these. But they ignore the teaching regarding the gifts in the same book. 1 Corinthians 13 is like the meat between the bread, and God gave us the whole sandwich to nourish and sustain us.

The gifts and fruit of the Spirit were never meant to be mutually exclusive aspects of the Christian life. Paul makes this clear: 'Follow the way of love and eagerly desire spiritual gifts' (1 Cor 14:1). 'Eagerly desire' is a strong verb; in Galatians 5:17 (av) it is translated *lusteth*. 'The flesh lusteth against the Spirit and the Spirit against the flesh.' God so means to fill the believer with his Spirit and love that, as he looks at the body of Christ, he is stirred by that same Spirit and love to prophesy.

I usually bring back a present for my wife if I have been away ministering for more than a few days. I could just return and say, 'My dear, I love you.' But when I express my love in a practical way and buy and give a gift, somehow it adds something to my words that helps her sense my love in a special way. This is an echo of what John says: 'Dear Children, let us not love with words or tongue but with actions and truth' (1 Jn 3:18).

If I see a friend working hard on his house, and it is possible for me to help him, it is not enough if I call out, 'My brother, I love you in the Lord. God bless you.' My love has a more real meaning if it has a practical expression.

The whole message of the three chapters in 1 Corinthians 12—14 is simply this: love with a gift. Love the body, using the gifts (charismata) to bless them. If we do not have this balance, a party spirit creeps in and divides us. Instead of the gifts or the fruit being the beautiful blessing God meant them to be, they become a point of division and an instrument in Satan's hand to divide the body of Christ. And as we saw earlier, it is rebellion: God hates 'a man who stirs up dissension among brothers' (Prov 6:19). These are manifestations of a party spirit: 'I am of Paul...I am of Apollos'; 'I am for the gifts'.... *Each one* needs the other to produce the balanced life that is pleasing to God.

An imbalanced life can be a symptom of rebellion. God has placed within us a variety of needs but has given provision to fulfil those needs in ways that help us to live a balanced life, glorifying him. These four basic needs, built into each of us are: the need to love and be loved, security, recognition and adventure.

To love and be loved

Being part of a Christian community enables this need to be satisfied. Through the working of the body of Christ, we have many opportunities to express love and care, and for God's love to be expressed towards us through others.

I remember one occasion when I was on my way with a car full of young people to a meeting. As we drove along the car began to fill with smoke and I just managed to switch off the engine and steer it into the forecourt of a garage, when it seized up altogether. I immediately realized that I could telephone any one of forty or fifty people and know a car would be there within ten minutes. I rang John, a local farmer, and of course he immediately came to our help. We can often take such love for granted, but on this occasion I felt humbled by the care God puts in people's hearts. Within minutes we were on our way again, with John's help, and each of us in the car were rejoicing because of that practical expression of kindness.

Security

Everyone needs to be secure. Often people build walls around themselves because of hurts and disappointments. They resist the security that comes through being a part of the family of God.

There was an occasion when I experienced insecurity. I had come under attack from one of the deacons in the church and I had gradually become obsessed with what was being done behind my back. Instead of trusting God to vindicate me in the situation, I let the situation undermine my confidence to the point where I was not effectively hearing God. I struggled on, not sharing this burden with anyone.

One Sunday, after the evening service, Bruce, the church secretary, came to my house. He had seen my struggles and confronted me with his observations about my inability, in recent weeks, to clearly preach God's word. Bruce's care for me was so great it overcame his fear of speaking so plainly and it broke through my defences. I was able to share the burden with him. I experienced the security that comes in having a brother who loved me and would stand with me and strengthen me in the battle.

Recognition

God has built into us a need for recognition. It was built into his own Son. Jesus needed recognition from his Father. When Jesus was baptized, the heavens were opened and the Spirit came down upon him like a dove. And there came a voice from heaven saying:

> You are my son whom I love; with you I am well pleased (Lk 3:22).

God has built the need into every human being. The Lord Jesus was *the* human representative. He needed recognition. Any parent knows that children need it too. But so do we. We do not need a falsely pious attitude to recognition. Rather, we need to learn to handle it in a way glorifying to God.

A few years ago when anyone said to me at the church door, 'Thank you, Barney, for that word,' I would say, 'Oh, don't thank me, give God the glory.' Then I read Keith Miller's book, *The Habitation of Dragons*. In it he pointed out that when someone compliments you and you respond with 'Give God the glory', you have, in a way, put that person down and elevated yourself. It is a false kind of humility.

God showed Keith Miller that when someone expressed appreciation to him, he should receive it and say, 'thank you.' Then afterwards he would bring that appreciation to the Lord and say, 'Father, you heard what that person said. Thank you for the privilege of being used to bless him.' He wants each one of us to appreciate and be appreciated. It is an aspect of the ministry of the body of Christ.

Adventure

The whole of life, when lived under the direction of the Holy Spirit, is an adventure. You never know what will happen next. God's word says:

> No eye has seen, no ear has heard, no mind has conceived what God has prepared for those who love Him (1 Cor 2:9).

God has a plan for each of our lives which unfolds as we walk with him:

> For we are God's workmanship, created in Christ Jesus to do good works, which God prepared in advance for us to do (Eph 2:10).

We have sent groups of young people from England and Canada to places overseas for exposure and ministry. They have been to Africa, India, Israel and Borneo and other places, too. This not only trains them in service but broadens their horizons through excitement and adventure.

You do not need to be either young or fighting fit to experience adventure! In small ways life for every Christian can be an adventure. Visiting new people, sharing our faith, exploring new places, exercising faith for our needs. When you invite one another for a meal, it can be an adventure for the guest—even more so when he or she is an elderly person.

Through his people in the body of Christ, God gives us opportunities to experience love, appreciation, security and adventure so we might be balanced.

9

Symptoms of Rebellion: Disobedience

Rebellion and disobedience are not synonymous. Rebellion has to do with an attitude of the heart and mind. Disobedience is to do with action. However, disobedience is a symptom of rebellion.

The whole of mankind came to be in a fallen state through what Paul calls 'the disobedience of the one man' (Rom 5:19). Paul then goes on to speak of mankind's redemption as being through the 'obedience of the one man.' One *Man*, doing just as he was told!

Disobedience is one of the main characteristics of the 'world', the kingdom of darkness. Ephesians 2:2 and 5:6 (NASB) refer to the world's people as 'sons of disobedience.'

In general, over the past century or so at least, people have not been trained to listen to God's word, read or spoken, with a view to *doing* it. God clearly included the word *obey* in the 'great commission' (Mt 28:19–20). Jesus was giving his disciples their final orders as to spreading the government of God over the earth. He did not say teaching them with brilliant sermons, or witty titles or subjects, or information or even only doctrine. He said:

> Therefore, go and make disciples of all nations, baptising them...and teaching them *to obey everything I have commanded you.*

The whole purpose of the going, proclaiming and teaching is to produce a people who have learnt obedience.

God's commands are not burdensome (1 Jn 5:3). We can in reality *delight* to do God's will (Ps 40:8). But unfortunately God's people today, generally speaking, tend to do their own thing. Even when they are busily engaged in 'serving' God it is on their own terms and in their own way. God does not want our efforts without a genuine submission of every area of our lives to him. He wants our zeal to be controlled and directed by the Holy Spirit.

If a group of people were only interested in sermon-tasting I would not be enthusiastic about being involved in pastoral care for them. Such people look to the dramatic and entertaining preaching but have little desire to hear the voice of God speaking into their lives, or ever to act upon it.

When people really listen to the word of God it can be compared to panning for gold in the stream of teaching. I am always encouraged when I see people listening closely to what is being said—even if the preaching is not polished or professional.

The word that is preached may cause a strong negative reaction. Often this happens when the light of God's word is piercing through to 'judge the thoughts and attitudes of the heart' (Heb 4:12).

When God's word challenges us to obey we often experience a subconscious negative response within. Barriers may be raised in defence, because, as Jesus said, 'Men loved darkness instead of light because their deeds were evil' (Jn 3:19). Attack or criticism may be one such self-defensive reaction.

When the word of God convicts a person in order to set them free, their initial reaction may be quite strong, touching, as it will, the subconscious strongholds where rebellion dwells.

In fact the one redeeming feature of rebellion is that it is not usually a deliberate act. It lies deeper and needs the light, a revelation from God, to bring it to the surface in order for the person to make a right response.

So when the word comes as an exposing beam of light, which we rarely welcome, or are drawn to, we can react not only to that particular issue, but often to some weakness or failure in the character of the one who brought the word.

For example, if you have been unfaithful to husband or wife, and the light is beginning to expose that, it requires a response of confession to clear it up and be forgiven. But a subconscious reaction is: 'No, if I let it out, I'm finished; my marriage is finished; my ministry is finished. I'll be rejected.' So one resists and reacts against the clear message from God.

An excellent rule of action is: weigh up any response you find in yourself which is angry or resisting. See what is behind it and judge yourself accurately. When the Spirit of God is operating through another servant of God to bring correction to me, it will, if right, come in patience, mercy and forgiveness. It will be with a view towards my being changed, or restored, so that I may be free to grow in God and be expanded in my ministry.

Such 'exposure' is out to bless me, not to put me down. So if my heart is looking for all that God has for me, there is no need to be defensive. I should welcome all the straightening out the Spirit seeks to bring about in me, because the fruit of the Spirit is 'love, joy, peace, patience, kindness, goodness, faithfulness, gentleness and self-control. Against such things there is no law' (Gal 5:22–23).

Here are three observations about disobedience before we look at the response of obedience.

God deals seriously with disobedience

1 Kings 13 tells the sad story of a man who was eminently used by God. In it we read of this man of God coming to Bethel as King Jeroboam was about to make an offering on the altar. The man cried out a strange prophecy against the altar:

> O altar, altar! This is what the Lord says: A son named Josiah will be born to the house of David. On you he will sacrifice the priests of the high places who now make offerings here, and human bones will be burned on you (v.2).

That same day the man also foretold a sign to prove his word true. The sign would be that the altar would be split apart and the ashes on it poured out.

When King Jeroboam heard what the man of God cried out against the altar at Bethel, he stretched out his hand from the altar and said, 'Seize him!' But the hand he stretched out towards the man shrivelled up, so that he could not pull it back. Further, the altar was split apart and its ashes poured out according to the sign given by the man of God by the word of the Lord.

Then the king said to the man of God:

> 'Intercede with the Lord your God and pray for me that my hand may be restored.' So the man of God interceded with the Lord, and the king's hand was restored and became as it was before (v.6).

The story spread through Bethel and was heard by another older prophet. He rode after the man of God till he found him sitting under an oak tree. He invited the man to come home with him and eat.

The man of God said:

> I cannot turn back and go with you, nor can I eat bread or

drink water with you in this place. I have been told by the word of the Lord: 'You must not eat bread or drink water there or return by the way you came' (v.16).

The old prophet answered:

I too am a prophet, as you are. And an angel said to me by the word of the Lord: "Bring him back with you to your house so that he may eat bread and drink water." (But he was lying to him.) (v.18).

So the man of God went with him. As they sat at the table the word of the Lord came to the old prophet. He cried out to the man:

This is what the Lord says: "You have defied the word of the Lord and have not kept the command the Lord your God gave you. You came back and ate bread and drank water in the place where he told you not to eat or drink. Therefore your body will not be buried in the tomb of your fathers." . . .

As he went on his way, a lion met him on the road and killed him, and his body was thrown down on the road, with both the donkey and the lion standing beside it (vv.20–22, 24).

Here was a man who carried the word of the Lord and was greatly used by him. Yet he disobeyed God's explicit instructions which he had clearly understood. So obedience in a prophet or leader anointed by God is a very serious thing to him. Read Deuteronomy 28, a striking chapter about the blessings of obedience and the 'curses' of disobedience for God's 'Old Covenant' people.

Disobedience is disrespect for God

Disobedience implies a disregard of the omnipotent, omniscient, omnipresent and eternal God. If we disobey, we are ignoring what God says, we are forgetting that he's watching, and we are assuming we can get away with it! But what is more, we are pitting our judgement against God's and saying that we think our way is better! It's an insult to him!

Disobedience includes omission as well as commission

We tend to stress the latter. We hear of a couple living together out of wedlock and realize they are disobedient. But if we omit to pray in a meeting when God has clearly prompted us, or omit to offer help when God tells us to—that is disobedience. Not to obey is as bad as being actively disobedient.

Now let us turn to obedience. How do we learn obedience? An obedient heart is one that continually listens to learn. It is a heart that seeks the will of God. There is the difference between *hear* and *heed*—called *hearken* in older English. Imagine that I am sitting at a restaurant table. A waiter is at the next table, receiving an order from the customer. Two people are listening to the customer's words, the waiter and me. I am merely curious: 'I wonder what he's going to have?' but the waiter, pencil and pad in hand, is listening with a view to doing. He's a servant and he is *heeding*. That should be our posture at all times, in relation to the authority of God.

How does God communicate his will to us? Basically in three ways:

Through his servants

Hebrews 13:17 says: 'Obey your leaders and submit to their authority.' God has placed leaders over each one of us in the body of Christ for the explicit purpose of conveying to us aspects of his will. It is dangerous to ignore their help or just to pick out advice that suits us.

Through his word

That is, both the *logos* and the *rhema*. As we have seen there is great danger in obeying only the *rhema*—a special word from the Lord in any given occasion. There is much Scripture that gives clear guidance on issues and this needs to be obeyed. Paul said to Timothy '*All* Scripture is...profitable...for training in righteousness' (2 Tim 3:16 NASB).

In our spirit

This is dramatically demonstrated when the gifts of the Spirit are exercised in a gathering. Less dramatic, but just as important, are the still, sure promptings we sense in our spirit. Practically speaking, this can be a sharp emphasis or strong impression but as we mature in God we learn to recognize his prompting. 'My sheep listen to my voice,' Jesus said.

In a public meeting the Spirit may prompt us to speak and, as a rule, it is better to be obedient to this even if we are a little uncertain or fearful of making a mistake. That was the sin of the man who buried his talent in the earth. The two others in the parable (Mt 25:14–30) risked what God had deposited with them, but this one was so careful not to make mistakes with his one little talent that he buried it. He took the easy way out but it resulted in him being sent to where there was 'weeping and gnashing of teeth.'

The Spirit of God says, 'Forget your pride. Be willing to take risks and make mistakes. Dare to step out on the water, because I am with you, and even when you begin to sink, and cry out, "Help me!", my hand is there to restore you.' I would rather be Peter, sinking, than the other disciples who were sitting in the boat not risking anything. I have learnt that although it is reassuring to have the support and help of others around, the Spirit of God sometimes draws us out upon a shaky limb, alone with him, but it is through those experiences that he teaches us to trust him.

I have also noticed that in learning to recognize the voice there is often this sequence of events. The first voice that we hear is the Spirit of God but is followed soon after by a whisper from Satan that causes us to doubt that voice. If our hearts are lifted in praise and worship and love for God and we sense him prompting us to pray or prophesy, we should take courage and step out. If we are wrong, and sometimes we may be, there should be enough love among God's people that we can cope with it.

Obviously if we continually mis-hear what God is saying, then it may need someone in authority in the gathering to point that out to us. This situation should be handled with gentleness and sensitivity so as not to crush the person who is spoken to. The aim of such correction should always be to see that person grow in understanding rather than be utterly devastated.

Obedience: the hallmark of a disciple

Peter calls his readers 'obedient children' (1 Pet 1:14) when he pleads with them not to conform to evil desires.

Paul has a striking compliment for the church at Rome:

> Everyone has heard about your obedience, so I am full of joy over you; but I want you to be wise about what is good, and innocent about what is evil.
>
> Now to him who is able to establish you by my gospel and the proclamation of Jesus Christ, according to the revelation of the mystery hidden for long ages past, but now revealed and made known through the prophetic writings by the command of the eternal God, so that all nations might believe and obey him—to the only wise God be glory for ever through Jesus Christ! Amen (Rom 16:19, 25–27).

This eloquently sums up God's plan and purpose for our lives: obedience.

Paul remarks in 2 Corinthians 7:15–16 how impressed Titus had been concerning the Corinthian church's obedience:

> His affection for you is all the greater when he remembers that you were all obedient, receiving him with fear and trembling. I am glad I can have complete confidence in you.

Obedience is so important if God is to be able to speak clearly to his church. If we cannot obey, God cannot command. So we will remain a rabble rather than an army until we learn to hear his commands. When we desire more than anything else to follow his orders, then we truly will be a part of the victorious army of God that will put the King's enemies under his footstool.

10

Bond-Slavery: The Key to Freedom

The rebellious heart is a stony heart. God wants to set us free from our rebellion and give us a new heart. Through the picture of the bond-slave we catch a glimpse of the new heart God wants to give us.

The Old Testament speaks of every fiftieth year being a 'Year of Jubilee'. Trumpets would sound throughout the land and all the slaves would be given the opportunity to be set free. Every slave would be given the choice: to live their life as a free man or to enter willingly into slavery again. If he did this he would be called a 'bond-slave'.

Originally the person may have become a slave as a consequence of debt. Perhaps he had a business that went bankrupt and because he could not pay his debt, he became the slave of the one to whom he owed the money. But when the Year of Jubilee came, it was reckoned by law that he had paid the debt and he was now free.

The slave, however, might face facts and conclude that freedom might mean starvation. There might be no prospect of an adequate living income. So he could go to his master and make a covenant with him, to become his bond-slave. From that day on, along with his family, he was the total property of his master. He relinquished any rights of his own. Even his wife and children belonged, in a sense, to his master.

As a seal of this covenant of bond-slavery the master would take him to the front of his house. Against the side post of the door he would pierce a hole through the man's right ear-lobe with an awl. From that day on he bore the mark of a bond-slave.

In Isaiah the Father speaks prophetically of Jesus and says:

> Here is my servant, whom I uphold, my chosen one in whom I delight; I will put my Spirit on him and he will bring justice to the nations. He will not shout or cry out, or raise his voice in the streets. A bruised reed he will not break, and a smouldering wick he will not snuff out. In faithfulness he will bring forth justice; he will not falter or be discouraged till he establishes justice on earth. In his law the islands will put their hope (Is 42:1–4).

Jesus was the perfect bond-slave, but instead of the ear-piercing, he was first baptized before he preached or healed. Baptism speaks very clearly of being dead and relinquishing one's rights. However, Jesus, of course, went much further. On the cross, his hands, feet and side were pierced, so in effect he bore all over his body the marks of a bond-slave.

The amazing thing about bond-slavery is not only that it is a way out of rebellion, but it is the way into infinite resources. At Jesus' baptism, the Father poured out the Spirit on him. This enabled Jesus fully to live out bond-slavery. We are told that he offered himself up 'through the eternal Spirit'; he did not do it himself. He did not have the resources to go through Gethsemane and Calvary on his own; they came from the Father and the Holy Spirit.

Jesus constantly repeated that he had no rights of his own when he was on earth:

I tell you the truth, the Son can do nothing by himself; he can do only what he sees his Father doing (Jn 5:19).

Paul spoke of this when he said:

Do nothing out of selfish ambition or vain conceit, but in humility consider others better than yourselves. Each of you should look not only to your own interests, but also to the interests of others. Your attitude should be the same as that of Christ Jesus: Who, being in very nature God, did not consider equality with God something to be grasped, but made himself nothing, taking the very nature of a servant, being made in human likeness. And being found in appearance as a man, he humbled himself and became obedient to death—even death on a cross! (Phil 2:3–8).

Jesus died on a cross because the Father told him to. Why did the Father tell him to do this? Because of the Father's love for his creation and for man.

Paul introduced his letter to the Romans in this way: 'Paul, a bond-servant of Christ Jesus' (Rom 1:1 NASB). There was no way he could have been called to be an apostle unless first of all he had become Christ's bond-slave.

Not everyone who claims to be a 'Christian' is a bond-slave. We read in Luke 14:25 that 'large crowds were travelling with Jesus'. But he doesn't want 'large crowds' merely as fellow travellers. So we read in the same scripture that he turned to them and said:

If anyone comes to me and does not hate his father and mother, his wife and children, his brothers and sisters—yes, even his own life—he cannot be my disciple (Lk 14:26).

The word *hate* is used here 'in comparison with his love for Jesus.' Jesus demands that he comes first.

Only three times in the New Testament do you find the word *Christian*, but 269 times the word disciple! We are called to be *disciples*! The great commission was to go and make disciples. We tend to use the word *Christian* very freely, for example, 'I met a lovely Christian the other day.' This term *Christian* was a kind of nickname, and given by the world. If we are to follow the emphasis of the Scripture, we would be better to say, 'I met a lovely disciple the other day.' We ought to start using this term! It's the one Jesus used. He never called anyone a Christian!

> Anyone who does not carry his cross and follow me cannot be my disciple (Lk 14:27).

Carrying your cross has to do with death, just as it did with the Lord. It has to do with bond-slavery, with denying yourself. It has to do with a practical understanding that when Jesus was crucified as a bond-slave, you were crucified with him. In baptism, moreover, you identify with Jesus as a bond-slave.

The marks of a bond-slave

Here are seven marks of a perfect bond-slave exemplified by the Lord Jesus.

A listening ear

> The Sovereign Lord has given me an instructed tongue, to know the word that sustains the weary. He wakens me morning by morning, wakens my ear to listen like one being taught. The Sovereign Lord has opened my ears, and I have not been rebellious; I have not drawn back (Is 50:4–5).

This clearly refers to Jesus Christ.

The well-known veteran missionary, Willie Burton, was one of the early giants of the Pentecostal awakening in this century. Willie, a great apostle of God, was responsible for the founding of nearly 1,500 churches in the Congo, in Africa. I was with him at a Baptist Youth

Centre when he shared his testimony with the chairman of the board responsible for the centre. He told of how he had been remarkably healed of cancer. The medical register in the hospital in Johannesburg, South Africa, had this entry: 'Mr Burton left this hospital today in a dying condition.' This was when Willie was in his forties. He died at the age of eighty-four! The fellow listened to the testimony, but when we left the room, Willie said to me, 'Brother, he didn't hear me.' 'You're right,' I said, 'he didn't.' The man's response was civil enough but there was no wonder in it. He was being a real English gentleman, not saying what he was really thinking. But, by contrast, Jesus had a sensitive and responsive ear and every morning he listened to his Father in order that, in what he did, he might please him.

Billy Bray was once asked, 'How often should one pray?' He replied: 'See that brass ornament? Every so often I give it a rub and that keeps it shining and bright. But if you leave it for long, it takes a lot of effort and time to polish it up again.' Jesus understood this principle. Jesus had that sort of relationship with his Father that kept him shining, and no tarnish could develop there.

When Aaron was set apart to be the high priest in Israel, an animal was slain and some of its blood was applied to three parts of the high priest: his right ear, right thumb and right big toe. The action spoke of being sanctified or set apart. His *ear* was set apart by God to listen. That came first. Then came the thumb signifying what he did and the toe signifying where he went.

What Jesus did and where he went was determined by what he heard. To know what it means to be a true disciple, we must cultivate that listening ear. This first mark of a perfect bond-slave unlocks all the other aspects.

Absolute dependence on the Father

Jesus gave them this answer: 'I tell you the truth, the Son can do nothing by himself; he can do only what he sees his Father doing, because whatever the Father does the Son also does. For the Father loves the Son and shows him all he does. Yes, to your amazement he will show him even greater things than these . . . . By myself I can do nothing; I judge only as I hear, and my judgment is just, for I seek not to please myself but him who sent me' (Jn 5:19–20, 30).

For I did not speak of my own accord, but the Father who sent me commanded me what to say and how to say it (Jn 12:49).

Jesus did not make judgements out of his own good ideas. When a situation needed a decision, Jesus said, 'Father?' and the Father gave him the answer, and so the decision was right. He was utterly dependent on the One who sent him.

Complete obedience

But the world must learn that I love the Father and that I do exactly what my Father has commanded me (Jn 14:31).

If you obey my commands, you will remain in my love, just as I have obeyed my Father's commands and remain in his love (Jn 15:10).

As Jesus obeyed, so he asks us to do the same. He asks nothing that he doesn't do himself, so in obedience Jesus is the perfect example. The epitome of his attitude is 'Your will be done.'

Full dedication to pleasing the Father

The one who sent me is with me; he has not left me alone, for I always do what pleases him (Jn 8:29).

Our Lord Jesus never did one thing that displeased his Father. Pleasing God was his meat and drink.

'My food,' said Jesus, 'is to do the will of him who sent me and to finish his work' (Jn 4:34).

Actually Jesus had every right to do his own will because he was co-equal with the Father. But he did not grasp that equality. He chose to relinquish all his own rights, to give himself totally to his Father to please him. Not only was the Father pleased, but he delighted in him.

Note that at Jesus' baptism in the Jordan in Luke 3:22 the Father said:

You are my Son, whom I love; with You I am well pleased.

God didn't call Jesus his bond-slave, but the Father said, 'You are my Son!'

The prodigal son returned as a servant to his father—ready to be a bond-slave—but the father said, 'No, you're my son.' 'For this son of mine was dead and is alive again; he was lost and is found' (Lk 15:24).

So *we* come to him as bond-slaves, as servants, but he treats us as sons of the Most High God.

Faithfulness

See to it, brothers, that none of you has a sinful, unbelieving heart that turns away from the living God (Heb 3:12).

In the high-priestly prayer, Jesus said:

I have brought you glory on earth by completing the work you gave me to do (Jn 17:4).

I asked one of my children to cut the lawn. He eagerly began with the electric lawnmower. But a friend came down the road and my son was distracted. Soon the sound of the mower ceased. He lost interest and was gone. He was a good starter but not a finisher. By contrast Jesus is 'the Alpha and the Omega,' the beginning and the end, the starter and the finisher.

> Jesus replied, 'No-one who puts his hand to the plough and looks back is fit for service in the kingdom of God' (Lk 9:62).

On the cross, he cried out with a loud voice, 'It is finished!' (Jn 19:30). This wasn't an exclamation of the life wrung out of him, it was a triumphant shout—*'It is completed!'* Jesus was as full of zeal at the end as he was at the start.

We need to be faithful and finish the work God gives us to do—with 'stickability', steadiness, steadfastness and resolve, for these are marks of a joyful bond-slave.

A serving attitude

> Jesus called them together and said, 'You know that the rulers of the Gentiles lord it over them, and their high officials exercise authority over them. Not so with you. Instead, whoever wants to become great among you must be your servant, and whoever wants to be first must be your slave—just as the Son of Man did not come to be served, but to serve, and to give his life as a ransom for many (Mt 20:25–28).

After his resurrection, Jesus could have come to visit his disciples in Shekinah glory with millions of angels accompanying him. Instead we see him, frying-pan in hand, cooking breakfast for his men.

There can be abuses of authority, but a true leader under God will not lord it over us or seek to force us to come under his authority. Jesus exercised authority in the right way. He did not even choose his own disciples but said: 'All that the Father gives me will come to me, and whoever comes to me I will never drive away' (Jn 6:37).

Look at the motley crew the Father gave him! Maybe Jesus wouldn't have chosen any, except perhaps John.

But it was not he, but his Father who did the selecting.

Humility

Once when I was in Yugoslavia, I had travelled some 600 miles on a sultry day, many of those miles along dusty roads. We finally arrived hot and weary at a little place called Panchievo, about 25 miles outside of Belgrade. As we were sitting there a man in his seventies came to us. He could not speak English, but he knew obviously that we were Christians. We exchanged "hallelujahs" (the one word that is the same in any language all over the world) while someone went to get an interpreter. This man, bless him, went and got a bowl of water. He would not even let us remove our own shoes and socks, and he began to wash our feet. It was one of the most beautiful experiences of my life.

Ted Kent, the man who was with me, told me the story of another man in that same village who had served him graciously. Ted had a weakness in his lung, so that if he got a cold it always developed into severe bronchitis and often pneumonia. He had had a severe cold and this man through the winter night constantly washed Ted's feet, placing them alternately on a hot and cold stone. Finally he worked that whole thing out of Ted. When he woke up in the morning, he was completely free of the cold. He told me that as this man was handling his feet, tears ran down his face. This Yugoslavian brother was loving and serving him. He said it was an experience he would never forget.

It is a custom in the East that your guest's feet be washed, and usually there is a servant to do it. But when the disciples met with Jesus on one occasion, there was no servant to wash their feet. They probably looked around at one another and thought, 'Who is going to do it?' It is not very comfortable to sit at a meal with unwashed feet in the East; it is like eating with unwashed hands. If you are lying in a reclining position on the floor at a low table, then your feet will be near the head of the person who is next to you.

John 13 says:

> Jesus knew that the Father had put all things under his power, and that he had come from God and was returning to God; so he got up from the meal, took off his outer clothing, and wrapped a towel around his waist. After that, he poured water into a basin and began to wash his disciples' feet, drying them with the towel that was wrapped around him.
>
> He came to Simon Peter, who said to him, 'Lord, are you going to wash my feet?'
>
> Jesus replied, 'You do not realise now what I am doing, but later you will understand.'
>
> 'No,' said Peter, 'you shall never wash my feet.'
>
> Jesus answered, 'Unless I wash you, you have no part with me.'
>
> 'Then, Lord,' Simon Peter replied, 'not just my feet but my hands and my head as well!'
>
> Jesus answered, 'A person who has had a bath needs only to wash his feet; his whole body is clean. And you are clean, though not every one of you.' For he knew who was going to betray him, and that was why he said not every one was clean.
>
> When he had finished washing their feet, he put on his clothes and returned to his place. 'Do you understand what I have done for you?' he asked them. 'You call me "Teacher" and "Lord", and rightly so, for that is what I am. Now that I, your Lord and Teacher, have washed your feet, you also should wash one another's feet. I have set you an example that you should do as I have done for you' (vv.3–15).

Again and again, we see in Jesus the perfect example of bond-slavery.

We are constantly encouraged to adopt the same attitude. Paul puts it clearly in Philippians 2:5–7 (NASB):

> Have this attitude in yourselves which was also in Christ Jesus, who although He existed in the form of God, did not

regard equality with God a thing to be grasped, but emptied Himself, taking the form of a bond-servant, and being made in the likeness of men.

Jesus humbled himself twice. By emptying himself of the prerogatives of deity and taking the form of a bond-servant, and by humbling himself to the point of death. In fact, Jesus in his humility became a very curse for us: 'Cursed is every one who is hung on a tree' (Gal 3:13).

Futhermore, in his trial Jesus did not defend himself:

He was oppressed and afflicted, yet he did not open his mouth; He was led like a lamb to the slaughter, and as a sheep before her shearers is silent, so he did not open his mouth (Is 53:7).

To those who misused and abused him, to those who hammered those huge, rough spikes into his hands, he said:

Father, forgive them, for they do not know what they are doing (Lk 23:34).

Jesus never asked his disciples to do anything that he had not done himself. When, for example, he said to his would-be disciples, 'Follow me,' he did not mean simply to fall in line behind him and go where he went. The word *follow* had a far deeper connotation: more to imitate or mimic. He was calling them to watch, imitate and duplicate his life.

Even Paul asked for the same attitude from those to whom he wrote. He said to the Corinthians, 'Be imitators of me, just as I also am of Christ' (1 Cor 11:1 NASB).

One day when I was a policeman, I was walking along Holloway Road in London in my policeman fashion. Policemen have a special style of walking; a kind of plodding along with their hands behind their backs. As I looked into the window of a large shop beside me, I saw, mirrored, a whole group of children behind me, walking just as I was. They copied my style, putting into action what they were seeing. Children love to mimic—that's how they learn. The principle is often used in teaching; for example, many teaching hospitals have an operating theatre so built that students can look down and see the surgeon at work. This is teaching by example.

So Jesus taught, constantly, by example. For although he was master of the crisp, clear spoken word in his teaching, it was his example coupled with the authority the Father gave him through the Spirit that was so significant, then and through the ages since.

We can hear the Father's words as he speaks:

Here is my servant [bond-slave], whom I uphold, my chosen One in whom I delight (see Matthew 3:17; 17:5).

Look at him, hear him and imitate him!

11

Freedom from Rebellion: The Next Steps

There is nothing easy or trouble-free about our walk with God. We are human, full of frailties and weaknesses, and we have determined enemies, spiritual hosts in the heavenly realms. We are prone to frequent failure. To grasp and experience God's grace and government in our lives we need to come to the end of ourselves. Only then can we relinquish control and submit totally to his rule. Nevertheless, God's purpose for each one of us is to use us fully in his kingdom in amazing ways. Here are four steps out of rebellion and into God's will for our lives:

1. Face Facts

God wants reality. When the prodigal son in Luke 15 asked his father: 'Father, give me my share of the estate.' He was really saying: 'Dad, I wish you were dead so that I could have the money. I can't wait for it so you can go on living and I'll clear out with the cash and leave you out of things.' But although there was rebellion and even un-reality there, he was ultimately brought to face facts. He reached rock bottom. For a Jew, to look after pigs is the lowest job you could ask for. Reality set in when he was reduced to eating pigs' food.

Then we read: 'He came to himself'—what marvellous words! A preacher in an open-air meeting stressed them dramatically by slowly taking off his top coat, jacket, shirt and finally his vest as he told the story. He pounded his bare chest when he shouted the words, 'He came to himself.' The prodigal's coming to himself seemed to clarify his situation. 'How many of my father's hired men have food to spare and here I am starving to death!' But the tragedy is that we often have to scrape the bottom of the barrel before facing facts.

We need to surrender our wills to God in the first place. His intention is not that we surrender only after circumstances have brought us to our knees, but like the bond-slave, he wants us continually to submit to him. He wants us to face the reality of the deep-rooted rebellion in us and lead us, step by step, out of that rebellion into a place of peace with him.

For us it may mean that we have drifted slowly away from God, our love grown cold and lost amid the clutter of our lives. Maybe we still read the Bible occasionally, and perhaps pray but we have lost the reality of the joy of his presence. Often it takes some tragedy or incident for God to get our attention again so that we face the facts of our situation.

Elijah ran away. Filled with self-pity, he went into a cave to escape from reality. God said to him, 'What are you doing here?' (1 Kings 19:9–18). Elijah, head in hands, felt desolate and alone. He felt that all was lost but God told him the real facts. He was not alone; there were 'seven thousand in Israel' who 'had not bowed down to Baal.' Elijah was a changed man.

As we face facts here are some questions that we need to answer:

Am I the centre of my life, or is Jesus the centre?

Who calls the shots?

Who's in charge?

Am I a self-pleaser or a God-pleaser?

Am I a giver or a taker?

Have I learned how to serve others, not in the way I

think they should be served, but in the way God says they should be served? (When some people 'serve' you wonder whom they have really served. Sometimes it's their own ego or need for fulfilment.)

Do I act presumptuously?

Am I doing good things which God has not specifically asked me to do?

Am I a fearful person?

Am I independent?

Do I find myself full of weariness, over-pressured?

Do I say things I wish I had not said?

Do I find myself saying things that don't bless or build up?

Am I, frankly, a self-willed, disobedient person, doing my own thing?

Do I find myself overly biased in one area of doctrine or behaviour in the church?

The first step then, is to come to yourself and face facts. One of the greatest dangers in the charismatic renewal is that people come to meetings week by week for a kind of pep-up, when they should be growing in the experience of carrying the presence of the Lord with them all the time, like a fragrance.

But thanks be to God, who always leads us in triumphal procession in Christ and through us spreads everywhere the fragrance of the knowledge of him (2 Cor 2:14).

God does not want us to be up and down, year after year, on an emotional high as a result of some corporate blessing only to sink down later into the stagnant pool of our inner lives. Thank God for our feelings, but feelings are not faith and we live by faith. 'The righteous will live by (his) faith' is said twice in the Bible: (Hab 2:4; Rom 1:17). Feelings should never blind us to reality and truth. The fact is that truth is often unpalatable to us because it means change. God knows this and so he reveals truth to us in stages so we can learn to handle it. Many still seek to avoid it.

I once heard Jamie Buckingham, a well-known Christian writer, make this quote: 'There is something too strong about truth for the human palate to receive all at once.' The reason, he said, was that truth always demands change; in fact, a full dose will actually put to death the old nature of man; therefore, rather than accept pure truth we choose to water it down, stone our prophets, or even believe an outright lie if it makes things easier. Novelists realize too much truth will cause the reader to reject their worth; thus, they build in hidden meanings to their stories. Just so, every serious teacher, especially the one who writes, suffers the same frustrations. He has something to say which will change the lives of his readers, yet he also understands that full exposure to the truth, especially if it cuts across the grain of some family tradition, financial motivation, or religious belief (and, you could add, personal preference) will cause many of his readers to reject both his truth and him personally. Stones, hemlock and crosses seem to accompany those who deal in the truth. Therefore, many like myself, are forced to give their readers little nuggets at a time, coating them with humour and imagery, hoping 'a little bit of sugar will make the medicine go down.'

Jesus, who taught in parables, once said to his disciples: 'I have much more I want to say to you, more than you can now bear' (Jn 16:12). What he was saying, in effect, is:

There are a lot of things I would like to tell you, things that would change your life and bring you happiness and abundance, but they would call for death to your old ways, even death to some of your religious practices, so I come in parables, hoping that you will go beyond them to seek the truth for yourselves.

The problem is often that we don't want to believe, because we will have to change.

2. Confess the truth about our rebellion

When the prodigal son came to himself and said, 'I will set out and go back to my father,' that in itself did not take him back. He had to get up and actually go, for the decision to do him any good. He could have sat and wallowed there in that pig-sty for weeks, munching on husks and saying: 'How many of my father's hired men have food to spare and here I am starving to death! If only I was to get up and go, things would be different!' Merely saying that would have changed nothing. He had to make a clear choice and act upon it.

After facing the facts, the next act the Bible requires is: confession. Reflect on the difference between King David and King Saul. David confessed his sin (2 Sam 12:13). When Nathan faced him with it, David said, 'It's true...' and went on later to write that sublime confession, recorded in Psalm 51, in which he asks God to create a clean heart in him and renew a steadfast spirit within him. Saul, on the other hand, when he was confronted with his sin said, 'It wasn't my fault; the people forced me to do it; Samuel didn't come on time' (1 Sam 13:11–12). He would not confess or take responsibility for what he had done. Saul made excuses. When faced with God's truth, people are quick to excuse themselves—no matter how clear the truth or evidence which confronts them. In fact, God will sometimes give people excuses not to believe because they would find excuses anyway.

For example, some Jews said that they did not believe in Jesus because: 'How can the Christ come from Galilee?' (Jn 7:41). 'But we know where this man is from; When the Christ comes, no-one will know where he is from' (v.27). Also they said, 'A prophet does not come out of Galilee'

(v. 52). Each of these cases, stemming from tradition, produced an excuse for rejecting Jesus as the Messiah. Matthew 13:14–15, tells us what Jesus said at one point about the people who were disbelieving and rejecting him:

> In them is fulfilled the prophecy of Isaiah: 'You will be ever hearing but never understanding; you will be ever seeing but never perceiving. For this people's heart has become calloused; they hardly hear with their ears, and they have closed their eyes. Otherwise they might see with their eyes, hear with their ears, understand with their hearts and turn, and I would heal them.'

John 12:37–43 tells us that God blinds those who do not want to see and hardens the hearts of those who do not want to understand.

If our hearts are basically unsubmissive then our hearing is impaired. Jesus said, in effect, to the Pharisees and scribes: 'You don't understand what I'm saying because you won't and can't hear me. Your own opinions, prejudices, traditions, speak so loudly that you cannot hear truth, even if you try. First be willing to do the will of God, unconditionally, whatever the cost, giving up your rights and preferences, then you will be able to hear and understand.'

This leads us to a very important key in the matter of dealing with truth. John 7:17 says: 'If any man chooses to do God's will, he will find out whether my teaching comes from God or whether I speak on my own.' The key is our attitude.

Sincerity is not enough. We need to choose to do God's will and, when he speaks to us, be willing to leave behind old ways even where we had previously sincerely felt them to be right. We need to surrender our will to the will of God. It is an essential prerequisite for understanding his truth.

The prodigal faced facts, came back to his father and confessed the truth:

> The son said to him, 'Father, I have sinned against heaven and against you. I am no longer worthy to be called your son.' But the Father said to the servants, 'Quick! Bring the best robe... put a ring on his finger and sandals on his feet. Bring the fattened calf' (Lk 15:21–23).

Did the father treat him like a bond-slave? No! He treated him like a son. Now, we do not presume on sonship. We don't come demanding sonship, with any arrogance or sense of right. We come humbly as bond-slaves. But if we do, wonder of wonders, we are treated as sons!

3. Make a clear choice for God

This means taking positive action on the word we have heard, just as the prodigal did. What is the choice we make? It's a choice for bond-slavery! The prodigal son thought of saying, 'Make me like one of your hired men.' We, too, need to express it out loud to the Lord. 'Jesus, I know it's going to be costly to be your bond-slave. It will be costly to be "a priest in my home" or to "make restitution to that person" or "submit to my husband" or "honour my parents".' May we pray, 'Lord Jesus, I come right now to be yoked to you. I take up my cross and put my neck in the yoke.'

These steps must be taken if we want to be free from rebellion and be able to live our lives in the joy of submission to our Saviour. It is not something we should do lightly or glibly. God sets the choices before us. He clarifies the issues but leaves us with the decision. Moses did this with the children of Israel.

> This day I call heaven and earth as witnesses against you that I have set before you life and death, blessings and curses. Now

choose life, so that you and your children may live and that you may love the Lord your God, listen to his voice, and hold fast to him. For the Lord is your life, and he will give you many years in the land he swore to give to your fathers, Abraham, Isaac and Jacob (Deut 30:19–20).

Joshua also gave Israel a similar ultimatum:

Now fear the Lord and serve him with all faithfulness. Throw away the gods your forefathers worshipped beyond the River and in Egypt, and serve the Lord. But if serving the Lord seems undesirable to you, then choose for yourselves this day whom you will serve, whether the gods your forefathers served beyond the River, or the gods of the Amorites, in whose land you are living. But as for me and my household, we will serve the Lord (Josh 24:14–15).

We have a clear choice before us. We are hearing God speak to us clearly in these days. We can either continue in rebellion, or come out of it. There is a tragic verse in Scripture that tells a story of how God's people chose once before in history. It says, 'Who were they who heard and rebelled? Were they not all those Moses led out of Egypt?' (Heb 3:16).

These people had been led out of bondage and out of Egypt. They had witnessed mighty acts of God as no other nation had. They experienced the supernatural power of God in their journey to a land of promise. Their shoes never wore out, they received manna from heaven and water in the middle of the desert. These people knew what it meant to praise God with song and dance and great celebration, yet they were people who were rebellious against God and his anointed authority; and so all of the men in that generation, with the exception of Joshua, Caleb and all the women, had to wander around in the desert until they died. The never got to see the Promised Land.

Jesus set a supremely clear line when he said:

> Come to me, all you who are weary and burdened, and I will
> give you rest. Take my yoke upon you and learn from me, for
> I am gentle and humble in heart, and you will find rest for
> your souls (Mt 11:28–29).

Jesus calls us to make a life-changing choice—to be yoked
to him. That is, to be a bond-slave. What Jesus is really
saying is, 'I am a bond-slave. Now you come and be yoked
to me. Put your neck where my neck is and we are going to
do it together on *my* terms in obedience to my Father.'
This will not be easy. Jesus knows that at times we all try
to go our own way, and that will be painful.

What you will really be saying when you make this
momentous choice is: 'All right, Jesus, I will put my neck
in your yoke. By whatever means you see fit, make sure I
keep in line with you. I'm giving you permission to chasten
and correct me—to make it very painful to step outside of
your will.' He knows it's the best way for us. To be yoked
to Jesus means rest and peace for our soul.

Frank Sinatra sang a song which epitomizes the spirit of
this age: 'I did it my way.' While I was in Canada I heard
the sad news of a girl who had taken her own life. The last
words she had written in her diary were: 'I have a choice:
God's way or mine—and I'm going mine.' Although she
was obviously depressed this comment shows how very
powerful our self-will is and just how final may be the
choices we make.

Jesus wants his song to be sung: 'I did it thy way.' 'Not
my will, but thine, be done' (Lk 22:42 RSV). Being a
bond-slave of Jesus means only wanting to do things his
way. This takes us into the next step.

4. Walk in continual obedience

Paul, writing to the church at Philippi says:

> Therefore, my dear friends, as you have always obeyed—not only in my presence, but now much more in my absence—continue to work out your salvation with fear and trembling, for it is God who works in you to will and to act according to his good purpose (Phil 2:12–13).

These verses give us a clear picture of what is involved in obedience.

The church at Philippi grew partly because they had learnt obedience through submission to Paul. It was through him that they were built up. They had also put into practice the word of God as it came to them. They took obedience very seriously. It is the Holy Spirit who draws us into obedience to God and it is the Spirit who strengthens us and enables us to continue to walk in that obedience.

Unfortunately many of us are unaccustomed to *doing* the word of God. We soak up spiritual knowledge like sponges, sermon after sermon, devotional after devotional, book after book, tape after tape, and we think we are really growing. But we are only growing in knowledge. Real biblical growth and stature is not how much you get into the word but *how much the word gets into you!* We are for the most part, giants in knowledge and midgets in experience.

This is not what God is after. In fact, the scripture says that if you only listen to the word and do not put it into practice you are deceived! Listen to James:

> Do not merely listen to the word, and so deceive yourselves. Do what it says (Jas 1:22).

There is a striking passage in the Old Testament where God speaks to the prophet Ezekiel.

> Mortal man, your people are talking about you when they meet by the city walls or in the doorways of their houses. They

say to one another, 'Let's go and hear what word has come from the Lord now.' So my people crowd in to hear what you have to say, but they don't do what you tell them to do. Loving words are on their lips, but they continue their greedy ways. To them you are nothing more than an entertainer singing love songs or playing a harp. They listen to all your words and don't obey a single one of them (Ezek 33:30–32 GNB).

Many people have a high regard for the Scriptures, and quite rightly so. But do we treat it as *God's* word, or are we like those people in Ezekiel's day who loved to come and hear what the Lord had to say as long as they didn't have to take it too seriously?

God quite clearly wants us to keep *all* of his word:

If you really keep the royal law found in Scripture, 'Love your neighbour as yourself,' you are doing right. But if you show favouritism, you sin and are convicted by the law as law-breakers. For whoever keeps the whole law and yet stumbles at just one point is guilty of breaking all of it. For he who said, 'Do not commit adultery,' also said, 'Do not murder.' If you do not commit adultery but do commit murder, you have become a law-breaker (Jas 2:8–11).

This scripture quite clearly says that God wants us to keep *all* of his word. We cannot accept some but excuse ourselves from other aspects, particularly where they touch important issues in our own lives. It is not valid to say to God: 'I'll do 80% of what you tell me, Lord, if you'll realize that I'm a human being; I have to have some leeway. After all, you don't expect me to be perfect, do you?' The answer is, yes, he is looking for perfection: for a stage-by-stage maturity.

In the past God's people have failed to walk in continual obedience. I believe it is going to be different in our times.

Thy people shall be willing in the day of thy power (Ps 110:3 AV).

This is certainly the day of God's power. We see his Spirit being poured out all over the earth, and are encouraged to believe that God's people will want to be willing and not rebellious in this day. We want, by God's grace, to come out of rebellion. We admit we have been hearers and not doers of the word. We see the need for doing it God's way, obeying him, being his bond-slave.

Jesus is coming back for a church that is holy and clean, 'without stain or wrinkle or any other blemish' (Eph 5:27). If we try to excuse ourselves when God puts his finger on something, we are guilty of not only breaking God's law, but also of rebellion.

In conclusion, here are three passages which show the infinite rewards of coming out of rebellion and into bond-slavery. The blessing of God is upon those who walk the road of obedience.

Do not merely listen to the word, and so deceive yourselves. Do what it says. Anyone who listens to the word but does not do what it says is like a man who looks at his face in a mirror and, after looking at himself, goes away and immediately forgets what he looks like. But the man who looks intently into the perfect law that gives freedom, and continues to do this, not forgetting what he has heard, but doing it—he will be blessed in what he does (Jas 1:22–25).

Jesus said:

He... who comes to me and hears my words and puts them into practice... is like a man building a house, who dug down deep and laid the foundation on rock. When the flood came, the torrent struck that house but could not shake it, because it was well built (Lk 6:47–48).

Blessed... are those who hear the word of God and obey it (Lk 11:28).

Epilogue

You may wonder why pride has not been mentioned as a symptom of rebellion. Pride is not a symptom, but rather a motivating factor which causes rebellion.

Pride was the reason for Satan's own fall from heaven. Ezekiel 28:17 says: 'Your heart became proud on account of your beauty, and you corrupted your wisdom because of your splendour.' He desired in his heart to be equal with God. This motivation caused him to rebel against his Creator and lose everything. Part of Satan's subsequent temptation to Eve in the Garden of Eden was to appeal to her ego—her pride. He told her that if she ate of the fruit she would not die as God had said, but rather she would 'be like God, knowing good and evil'.

The answer to pride is to humble ourselves under the mighty hand of God (1 Pet 5:6), and through submission to him to discover our true calling and identity as children of God.

Restoration in the Church

by Terry Virgo

God is restoring his church. Many are now seeing the need to apply New Testament principles to their church structures and time-honoured traditions. Flexibility and freedom are on the increase.

This book takes an inside look at what has been called 'the house church movement' and reveals how amazing growth has come from a rediscovery of Scripture's teaching on ministries in the church. Whatever our situation, we will find a fresh challenge in what the author has to say.

☐ The traditional evangelical is reminded that restoration is rooted in the orthodox teaching of the Reformers.

☐ The charismatic is asked not to stop with personal gifts but to go on to embrace the ministries of apostle and prophet.

☐ Those already committed to restoration are urged to be watchful, avoiding complacency and ready to move on to whatever God has in store.

Terry Virgo is based at Clarendon Church, Hove, Brighton. A frequent visitor to many countries with the message of restoration, he is highly respected for his ministry to church leaders in various denominations, and is a popular speaker at Bible Weeks each year. He is married with five children.

k
Kingsway Publications